Freemasonry in Black and White Myths and Facts: Popular and Unpopular

Author
Charles M. Harper Sr.
Foreward by Mir Omar Ali
Edited by Rossitza Meek

"True wisdom comes to each of us when we realize how little we understand about life, ourselves, and the world around us."
Socrates

Freemasonry in Black and White
Copyright © 2013 Charles M. Harper Sr. All rights reserved. No part of this work may be reproduced, stored in a retrieval system or transmitted, in any form or by any means, electronic, mechanical, photocopying, recording, or otherwise, in whole or in part, without the express written consent of the Author
Printed in the United States of America

ISBN 10 is 0615819060
ISBN 13 is 9780615819068

Book Reviews-

"I was lucky enough to read an advance copy of this work. It is not just a well-written work, it is valuable to the education of every Freemason. I am better for having read this work and strongly encourage all Masons to do likewise." - Michael R. Poll, New York Times best-selling author, owner of Cornerstone Publishing, Fellow and Past President of The Masonic Society, a Fellow of the Philalethes Society, a Fellow of the Maine Lodge of Research and Secretary of the Louisiana Lodge of Research.

"This book is not for the faint of heart. ...Just the way in which this Brother came to Masonry makes for a fun Masonic television movie...it was quite the ride and he has the courage to share what he learned along the way. Race, clandestine Masonry, mysticism, etc. All included. I enjoyed the journey with him and can recommend the read." – Cliff Porter, author of *The Secret Psychology of Freemasonry*, *Masonic Baptism*, and a noted national lecturer and instructor in the field of subconscious communications.

There is no national or international Masonic authority. Freemasonry in North America is governed by independent legislative bodies known as Grand Lodges who exercise absolute Masonic authority within a state or province.

Writers may express their opinions about the Fraternity, but their statements are not authoritative. Only Grand Lodges can make authoritative statements, and these apply only to their members. (Prepared by the Masonic Information Center, March 2001)[i]

In these pages, I express my opinions alone, developed through research and experience. In no way, do they express, or allude, to the opinions of any Masonic Grand Lodge, Lodge or Masonic Body.

---

[i] http://www.msana.com/focusarchives/focusapr01.asp

Table of Contents

Foreword

While many have attempted to encapsulate the nature of Freemasonry into a single expression, very few have succeeded. In every so-called description or definition of the Craft, however, there is one common trait: its Universality.

The "Universality of Masonry" not only refers to the reaches of its moral and philosophical teachings, but also to the composition of its membership. The journey of the Masonic Craft aside from its degrees, perspectives, fellowship, and benevolent action, offer a unique experience to the initiate undergoing the transformation it offers.

The nature of this experience goes to the very heart of the masonic purpose and the secrecy therein contained. While one may be able to find numerous publications on the work, rituals and philosophies of the craft, often including the so thought "secret" modes of recognition, these hardly constitute the essence of Freemasonry. Context is what gives any component meaning, and that context is only to be found in the heart of a sincere initiate forthrightly receiving the initiatory work and employing the tools provided him therein to grow and facilitate his own enlightenment. It is accordingly revealed that the true nature of Freemasonry is intangible, and its "secrets" can never be truly "revealed," but only understood amongst the brethren of the Craft.

Furthermore, the experience a man endures as he is transmuted from a "profane" or rude substance, and is crafted into the "sublime" nature of a mason, provides him the tools with which to labor and the eyes to "see." The externals of masonry consisting of its written words, ceremonies, and the like, form its exoteric shell while the intangible forms of its being borne in the heart of a true follower, forms the esoteric constitution that enables one to take the key, employ it, and walk through the door towards their sublime goal.

The universality of Masonry spoken of here is ever present in the diversity of its membership and the varying levels of perspective each has about their relationship to and understanding of the order. It is the crux of being unique as individuals that in fact makes us all the same, meeting on the level and exhibiting the core of a true brotherhood. Freemasonry in Black and White offers an incredibly unique insight into this uniquely "masonic" experience. The narrative, from the specific perspective of one brother, enables the reader to gain an understanding and appreciation for what it is that masons have been doing from time immemorial, continue to do today and shall do for perpetuity into the future.

The picture here presented offers insight that is relevant both to the masonic member and the non-mason. In addressing common misconceptions about the fraternity, one finds a resource for those outside the craft to learn its true purpose while providing a wealth of answers for its own members to provide those asking such questions. The book's narrative, offered from a single man's point of view in the craft, offers other brethren a perspective other than their own while enabling a non-mason to catch a glimpse into the fraternity through a member's eyes. As a final thought, it leaves the reader with a commentary on the current condition of masonry and where it can progress from here about innovation, and more importantly, restoration.

The Ancient and Honorable Fraternity of Freemasons is an organization that has gone through many transformations since its formal founding in the eighteenth century, its emergence as a guild prior to that and the traditional histories that remove it to even further antiquity. Throughout this history, masonry has endured evolution as societies progressed and misconception and conspiracy fueled anti-masonic sentiment. On every occasion the

Masonic Craft has exhibited its resilience and adaptability, and as a phoenix from the ashes, has always risen again. This book is an example of the increasing scholarship of the membership of the current time and is among many new waves of masonic thought and exploration that will propel our craft and its members into the new millennium. Freemasonry is a journey towards an ideal, a journey in which it enables its members to acquire the means with which to think critically and without prejudice, and therefore perpetuate the ultimate power of reason and ideas. Freemasonry in Black and White is a marvelous addition to the myriad of expositional work that forms contemporary masonic thought and illustrates the fortitude that defines the modern masonic identity.

"Philosophy is a kind of journey, ever learning yet never arriving at the ideal perfection of truth"
- Albert Pike

Right Worshipful Brother Mir Omar Ali
Member of the Board of Grand Examiners
Grand Lodge of AF&AM of Illinois

Preface

"Freemasonry is a gift, not a privilege." These are the words of the 2011-2012 Most Worshipful Grand Master of the Ancient Free and Accepted Masons of the State of Illinois, Most Worshipful Brother Terry Seward, at a Town Hall meeting I attended once in 2012. Before that night, I had not thought of Freemasonry in that way. I knew it was special and not every man could be a member, but I had not considered it in that context before.

Then again, my journey into Freemasonry is a little atypical. You see, I began my Masonic journey as a member of what I later discovered to be was a clandestine lodge. When I use this term, I am not speaking of two regular Grand Lodges that have withdrawn recognition from one another, as we are regard any Grand Lodge without formal recognition with our own, but one that was never formed in a regular manner at all. This did not mean that the members were bad people; in fact, quite the contrary. Several members of the former St. Elmo Lodge no. 70A of Kankakee, Illinois, were remarkable men, and wanting the best for their community, and desired to make good men better. They were simply misinformed, or understood differently, as to what defines a Lodge to be regular, and so existed outside mainstream Freemasonry.

To add to the complexity of the situation, my father is a member of a Prince Hall Affiliated Grand Lodge in Illinois. My mother is a member of the Order of the Eastern Star, Prince Hall Affiliated of Illinois, and both are regular Masonic Jurisdictions. Prince Hall Affiliated Masons have had to deal with clandestine Masonry in the urban community since the late 1800's, as they were misleading men into their organizations for the dishonorable purposes of making money. Here I was, their son, and a member of the very groups regular Masons frown upon.

I had no idea at the time the direction my life would head in the discovery of the membership of which I held in the clandestine Lodge, and the things I would be challenged to overcome in the way I dealt with finding a resolution to end this dilemma. I was a clandestine Mason. I was seeking membership into a Caucasian Mainstream Masonic Lodge. And, all the while, being a man of Bi-racial heritage. Some would probably question what a man's ethnicity would have to do with being a Freemason where it is constantly stated that it is the universality of man under the fatherhood of God, and it is the interior and not the exterior of man, that is judged for membership. The details of the relevance to ethnicity is later to be explained.

This expedition in truly discovering the nature of my Masonic association, the road to researching the procedure to become a regular Freemason, who I was to become in terms of spiritual and mental growth, and the maturation process I would undergo, would prove to make my journey that much more rewarding. Everything I knew about Freemasonry and my own morality, would be examined. I would call into question what I previously defined in terms of the rules of how to live before becoming a Freemason, what I believed was a life of high quality, moral, and ethical uprightness afterwards my initiation, how I became endowed with true humility, and finally how I learned and grew the effort to obtain and maintain a positive life.

The purpose of this book is not to define what constitutes Freemasonry for any Grand Lodge, any Lodge of any Grand Lodge's jurisdiction, or any individual Mason himself. It is not to argue that any Lodge or Grand Lodge existing outside of formal recognition with my own Grand Lodge should be regarded as clandestine by any other jurisdiction in any way, for each Masonic jurisdiction judges by its own constitution and by-laws whom it chooses to recognize as Masonic, and who it does not. This book is also not to say that any jurisdiction promotes a division amongst the ethnicities that might comprise its membership.

This book is intended to bring to light issues that do exist as I have experienced them: negativity, racism within lodges, and the unintentional misrepresentation of Masonic history; and positively, a renewed spirit in Masonic brotherhood. It is to promote discussion of possible solutions to issues that are not usually spoken about amongst different Brethren as it is considered taboo, or at least in bad taste, because they involve topics troubled history, undesirable memories, and difficult emotions. These things tend to impede the process of logical thought, and inhibit the process of productive conversations amongst Brethren.

But in a speculative Masonic Lodge amongst Brethren, one is encouraged to bring to light thoughts that could make men better. In that spirit, I wish to convey my voice to all who may consider them in the same sincere manner as one Mason should communicate with another in public, as well as in private, in the friendliest manner. A Mason should communicate words that may aid in defining our problems and developing solutions. Only when we bring to light those issues that fester in the dark, can we dispel them, and together, uplift the greatest gift to humanity; the goodness that exists within us all.

Introduction

I am a Freemason

ii

ii This photo was taken by Brother Jammie Shell, a member of Kankakee
Lodge No. 389, in Portsmouth, Ohio, during the Black Watch tour of the
Grand Lodge of Scotland.

I am a Regular Master Mason from the State of Illinois. Am I unique? No. Are there unique experiences in the journey I have taken to become a Mason? Yes. Am I someone special? No. Have the situations I have been confronted with, and the choices I have made, created a special experience for me? Yes. But, that is just it. There are many men are seeking enlightenment in the Fraternity of Freemasons, but not all have taken the regular beaten path in becoming one. It is the reflection of their journey, seen through light measured within due bounds of their true definition of morality with the compasses, that can allow them to see the light of their journey and share this with others. This book is my personal experience of this journey.

In 1775, a man by the name of Prince Hall sought entry into a Freemason's Lodge in Boston, Massachusetts. Prince Hall was not a white or black man, he was both. Born to a French mother and a Haitian father, he was a freed slave of bi-racial decent, a mulatto by the terms of 18th century America. Defined by Merriam-Webster Dictionary, a mulatto is, or was depending on your personal feelings of the word, the "first-generation offspring of a black person and a white person or a person of mixed white and black ancestry."[iii] I am considered a mulatto, having a black father and a white mother.

[iii] http://www.merriam-webster.com/dictionary/mulatto

Like Prince Hall, I was not raised with this identity. Most African-Americans will tell you that if you have a drop of black blood in you, then you are black. The "one-drop rule was a racist device to ensure that slaveholder's multiracial children remained slaves."[iv] I digress. Though Prince Hall had a white mother, he was considered a black man. And as such, he was not allowed to join a white Masonic lodge in 1775 America, where slaves were merchandise and could not be equals, as Masons treat one another, "on the level" as we say.

So, what were Prince Hall's alternatives? He desired to become a part of this Fraternity were men of stature belonged and were given respect in the community. George Washington was a Freemason and led the war of Independence for the United States. Benjamin Franklin was a Freemason and assisted in gaining France's assistance for the fight for independence.

[iv] Jandt, F. 2013. An Introduction to Intercultural Communication:

Identities in a Global Community. Sage Publications, Inc.

Prince Hall was an abolitionist. He sought to free blacks from slavery, establish schools for blacks to become educated and even petitioned Congress to abolish slavery. Becoming a Freemason was a way to assist in this cause.

The alternative for Prince Hall was to petition a Lodge under the jurisdiction of the Grand Lodge of Ireland, Lodge No. 441 to be exact. In this Lodge, he and 14 other men of color were made Master Masons with all the rights and privileges of one, within the jurisdiction of the Grand Lodge of Ireland. As told by Brother Robert C. Blackburn in 1991's Grand Lodge of Ireland's History, "In 1775, Lodge No. 441, attached to the 38th Foot in Boston, initiated Prince Hall and fourteen African-Americans into Freemasonry. It was through an Irish Masonic lodge; therefore, that "Prince Hall" Masonry came into being."[v] It seemed that the only way for Prince Hall to become a Freemason would be to join a Lodge with liberal and progressive minded men who did not see the color of one's skin or their heritage as a means of denying admittance to these enlightening teachings.

However, when the regiment left Boston, Prince Hall's Lodge was only left with the rights to march on the Masonic holiday of St. John's Day and bury their dead with Masonic Rights. This was not enough for Prince Hall and the 14 other men of his Lodge. Prince Hall sought out more freedom to travel masonically, and legally advance the benefits of Masonic knowledge for all men of color. He would have to reach all the way across the Atlantic Ocean to get this permission by the way of a Charter from the Grand Lodge of England for the first African-American Lodge, African Lodge No. 1. Prince Hall's efforts showed that there is no distance to far to reach in gaining what one seeks.

---

[v] http://www.irishmasons.com.sg/concf/index.php/history

Having said all of that, my relation to Prince Hall's efforts is one of understanding and inspiration. America, though a great country of democracy and freedoms, is not without dark periods a race conflict, specifically three most notable periods: slavery, from the establishment of the first settler's in the 1600's and the establishment of these United States from Great Britain in 1776, the Civil War in 1861and the Civil Rights Movement that culminated in the passage of the Civil Rights Act of 1963. 2012 is not a year that is far removed from the negative feelings, in both black and white cultures, passed down through generations of slave owners and slaves, the Union and the Confederates, and from those that were pro-segregation, and those against it.

The Fraternity of Freemasons and its members, and each individual lodge being a microcosm of society of which it draws its membership, and though firmly against racism and the limitation of free ideas, is not without members that may quietly harbor feelings that have no logical basis, but were generationally taught and handed to them, and subconsciously act on these ideas with their own judgments. For the last two centuries, blacks have had Prince Hall Lodges and whites had their own, the Most Worshipful Prince Hall Grand Lodges and the state Grand Lodges of the United States, respectively. Until 1989, the state Grand Lodges would not recognize Prince Hall Masons as Freemasons period, until finally a resolution by the Grand Lodge of Massachusetts permitted the establishment of a recognition compact.

These ideologies through time would not just have constant ripple effects on the state level, but effects that reverberated down to each individual lodge and the potential members. It would lead to a rise of clandestine black lodges in the mid-1800's that have existed since then, and has produced more numbers even today, primarily within large cities of the United States. It would lead to confusion of black men seeking to become Freemasons, steered away from the predominately all white lodges by the threat of exclusion based from race and seeking admittance to any black lodge seen to have the emblem of the Fraternity attached to it, legally established or not. It would lead to fighting over the authority of which black Grand Lodges were legally formed and which were not. This fight that started in the late 1800's and still exists today between non-recognized black Grand Lodges and the formally recognized Prince Hall Grand Lodges in the United States.

Education on many issues of the Fraternity, its history, who can become a member and who cannot and how, has found its way into homes due to the desire of the Fraternity to educate the public to who the Freemasons are and what they do. But the arrival of Freemasonry on the internet has been both good and bad for the Fraternity.

It is good because it has made available information on what the purpose of Masonic Lodges are and where they are located. Also, it tells men of the petitioning process and provides pictures of who Masons are and what they look like. It shows Masons of every race and creed in a Masonic Lodge standing shoulder to shoulder with one another. It combats the old idea of a "white only" or a "black only" lodge. It shows Prince Hall Lodges with other ethnicities as members and it shows the former white only lodges with many different ethnicities in their membership.

This is an advertisement by a clandestine Grand Lodge in Chicago, Illinois in 2012, the Grand Lodge of Amen Ra. It was used to promote the public to pay ten dollars apiece for the same information available for free on the internet. Notice in the picture there is no Grand Lodge stated and no Lodge name stated, yet this is done in the name of Freemasonry. How would a person that is not knowledgeable about Freemasonry be aware that this is not permissible by a regular Grand Lodge? This advertisement was placed in a Facebook chat-room. A man by the name of Albert Higgens-El placed the advertisement and stated the name of the Grand Lodge as the Grand Lodge of Amen Ra which had created a "Masonic University." This Grand Lodge was incorporated in Illinois on November 7, 2003 by Silvia M. Brewer, file number 63174483.

As much as the internet has been good for the Fraternity, allowing Masonic Brethren from opposite sides of the world to communicate where they may have never met otherwise, it also has been bad for the Fraternity. It has given a voice to clandestine lodges who feed on the old feelings of America's dark past of racism and sexism. Black clandestine lodges feed into this by promoting that whites have taken black peoples ancient knowledge and they have retrieved it to share with other blacks. Clandestine lodges such as co-masonry, prey on ideas of inequality, promoting that it is not equal if women are not included. Both ideas are fallacies.

I must note that there is no such thing as a black or white lodge. It has been categorized as such in the past due to the history of the United States, but that time has passed as many Masons have sought, and continually seek, to remove this

---

vi A Cairo Masonic lodge in the 1940s, under a portrait of King Farouk

negative aspersion, promulgated by ignorance, from the face of the Fraternity. It does not mean that racism may not still linger in the hearts of some men, black and white, but the stem of intolerance and confrontation of these ideas publicly or privately displayed, has risen incredibly since the formal recognition of the Most Worshipful Prince Hall Grand Lodge of Massachusetts and white and black masons began to inter-visit and fellowship with one another in regular tyled lodges.

My experience is one that has brought me from almost joining my father's Prince Hall Lodge in 1998 by petitioning and then deciding I was not mature enough to join the Fraternity and potentially harm my father's good name, to joining a clandestine black lodge in 2004. Unbeknownst to me what a clandestine lodge even was, I finally petitioned and received membership in a predominately white lodge in 2010 and since have been truly enjoying the rights and privileges of a regular Master Mason.

My journey has been a truly educational one, spiritually, socially and when finally binding the two together, masonically enlightening. It is a story of a man born of a black father and white mother in the 1970's in Chicago, Illinois, having the complexion of a white man, raised as a black man, and then learning to find the best of both worlds within myself. It is a journey of finding identity and purpose, failure and success as a father, son, husband, sibling, friend, and finally, as a Freemason.

In the story that I convey in this book, I must inform those that choose to read this book and take the journey the words will truly carry you, there will be no Masonic secrets told here, just inspiration for the path if one chooses. There will be no purposeful disgracing of men that I have come to know in my journey. It is not a book to sway anyone for, or against, their free choice of the path they must choose of their own free will and accord to travel in hopes to obtain self-enlightenment. I am a Master Mason, obligated as one, and I will uphold my obligation taken in front of my Brethren and my Deity, to perpetuate the goodness of our Fraternity. This story will simply be the truth as I have experienced it, and the description of the inspiration and courage it has given me to speak of my conclusions.

This journey of shared experiences and knowledge gained is to inform the misinformed. It is to dispel myths of the Fraternity. It is to confront racist views through education of personal experience and substantiated facts. So, buckle in, open your third eye, and please digest the information and grow your insight. Seek that which all as Freemasons do, truth without veils of illogical rhetoric, without the cast of oppressive viewpoints, and without politically correct statements. This is my story, Freemasonry in black and white, the myths and facts of a journey to self-enlightenment.

Chapter 1

The Purpose of Freemasonry

The Public's Misconceived Purposes

There always seems to be public speculation about the true intent of the Fraternity of Freemasons. Are they good or are they bad? Do they have plans to take over the world under the auspice of a "New World Order," so commonly heard of on talk radio stations or commented on by conspiracy theorists anywhere one may look on the internet? More importantly, what are they doing in those Lodges behind closed doors? The most popular connection of Freemasonry is to the Illuminati. Let us explore the origins of these misconceptions and place them against credible and substantiated facts.

Generally, Freemasonry's purpose is to unite men and "make good men better" using initiatic rituals that exemplify, through both physical actions and philosophically spoken meanings, the examples of honor, integrity, sacrifice and deceit. The intent of this experience is to impress upon the mind of a man the necessity of always seeking to improve himself in conscious thought, resulting in better actions or deeds. This ritual, spoken by mouth-to-ear, since time immemorial, and originally written by William Preston in 1776 in the book, 'Illustrations of Freemasonry' captures examples of the deepest thinking from amongst the greatest societies that has ever existed, and a form of it is used in every Grand Lodge in the United States.

It must be noted that the Preston-Webb rituals, the combination of Preston's work and re-written to Americanize it by Thomas Webb, is used predominately as a basis for all the United States Grand Lodge rituals, but it is not the only authorized masonic rituals written or used in all Lodges in the world, or all jurisdictions of the United States. There exist rituals said to have existed in France before those used in the English Constitutions, and it is encouraged that all should do more research on these rituals used predominately outside the United States in Masonic Jurisdictions that authorize the Scottish Red Degrees. More information can be found on the philosophy of these degrees by reading *Morals and Dogma of the Scottish Rite Craft Degrees* by Albert Pike, which can be found published by Brother Michael R. Poll of Cornerstone Publishing.[vii] Brother Poll has done extensive research into the origin of these degrees and of those jurisdictions in the world that authorize its use.

This is not to say that this was the only ritual written by 1776 in London, England, but it was the only ritual authorized to be written by the Grand Lodge of England. There were many exposés written to expose the secrets of the Freemasons, and to make a profit from the existence of the Fraternity. These written rituals, catechisms, were notes taken from the memory of men who either at one time were Masons, or from those who heard stories of what transpires in a Masonic Lodge.

Freemasonry has become popular in the mainstream culture due to movies recently made such as '*National Treasure*' and '*The Da Vinci Code*,' both using instances of truth and fiction to create an interesting story for the audience. As both movies, and others of course, display Freemasonry in an intriguing and mystic fashion, hidden codes and secrets, there is yet another fashion in which Freemasonry has caught the eye of the mainstream society. Music icons of pop culture have started to use the mysticism to gain popularity.

Hip-hop stars have begun using masonic symbols such as the square and compass in both their lyrics and in their clothing brands. Jay-Z, a rap star and entrepreneur, has developed a clothing line known as Rocawear, which has hats, pants and shirts that bear the symbol and a label that states, "Masters of the

[vii] http://www.lulu.com/shop/albert-pike-and-foreword-by-michaelr-

poll/morals-and-dogma-of-the-scottish-ritecraftdegrees/

paperback/product-1211287.html

Craft," under the logo. He boasts lyrics in a song by hip-hop rapper Rick Ross called Freemason that says, "…I said I was amazing Not that I'm a Mason It's amazing that I made it through the maze that I was in Lord forgive me I never would've made it without sin…"[viii] Though both of these artists have stated publicly through many media outlets that they are not Freemasons, it has not stopped the culture that listens to hip-hop from purchasing anything that has the perception of Freemasonry and wearing them as a fashion symbol.

[ix]

Though neither this hat nor symbol is authorized, or publically supported by any regular Masonic Grand Lodge, it has not stopped the anti-masonic crowd from attaching the name

[viii] http://music-row.ru/blog/rick_ross_free_mason/2010-08-08-993

[ix] http://www.strictlyfitteds.com/blog/2011/04/rocawear%E3%80%8C

wool%E3%80%8Dfitted-baseball-cap

"Freemason" to these rap stars, and with the content of the lyrics of these songs, and of these artists, and manipulating the lyrics as a statement from the Masonic fraternity. This, however new of an occurrence, is not the first time a person has used the mysterious nature of the fraternity of Freemasonry as a source for financial gain.

Samuel Prichard was one such supposed Mason who wrote and published these rituals of initiation, passing and raising of a Mason in 1730 in a book entitled, "*Masonry Dissected.*" Prichard states that he was a Freemason of a Constituted Lodge in London on the cover of his book. Noted Masonic Author Albert Mackey wrote about Prichard in his book entitled *Encyclopedia of Freemasonry*, "This work, which contained a great deal of plausible matter, mingled with some truth as well as falsehood, passed through a great many editions, was translated into French, German and Dutch languages and became the basis or model on which all subsequent so-called expositions, such as Tubal-Kain, Jachin and Boaz, etc., were framed."[x]

There have been many notable exposures of Masonic ritual over the years. The most recently notable one is that of Malcolm C. Duncan's, *Duncan's Masonic Ritual and Monitor*, published in 1866. Duncan states that the purpose of his work is, "Not so much to gratify the curiosity of the uninitiated as to furnish a guide for the neophytes of the Order, by means of which their progress from grade to grade may be facilitated."[xi] While Duncan states that he is attempting to educate the uneducated Mason, what he accomplishes is the same as Prichard, he attempts to publically expose ritual of the Fraternity in hopes to make a financial profit.

---

[x] Mackey, A. 1873, Encyclopedia of Freemasonry, Moss and co. pg. 800

[xi] http://legende-hiram.blogspot.com/2010/07/blog-post_22.html

What Prichard, Duncan and others including the Rap artists have done, is negatively affected the purpose of the Fraternity. Instead of putting the members of the fraternity's time and energy into educating men and conducting charity, energy must be continually diverted to educate the public and thwart misconceived ideas of the Fraternities purpose. The effect of the attempt to release "secrets," has empowered the anti-Masonic crowd to take the words and manipulate their meanings to fit their agenda. The negative domino effect of this is not only the responsibility of answering questions that have nothing to do with the purpose of a Masonic Lodge to the public, but having to dispel unsubstantiated claims in hopes of removing negative aspersions of the Fraternity. These aspersions, or unsubstantiated ideas, have a negative effect on potential membership.

The Illuminati is often associated with Freemasonry as well. From the stories containing mystery of years gone by, to the pop culture making constant references to the Illuminati by rap stars, the inclusion of the fraternity and this group from Bavaria is consistently linked. The Illuminati, started in Bavaria by a gentleman named Weishaupt, was a "secret organization, comprising schools of wisdom, concealed from the gaze of the world behind walls of seclusion and mystery, wherein those truths which the folly and egotism of the priests banned from the public chairs of education might be taught with perfect freedom to susceptible youths."[xii]

By the constitution of an order whose chief function should be that of teaching, an instrument would be at hand for attaining the goal of human progress, the perfection of morals and the felicity of the race. On May 1, 1776, the new organization was founded, under the name of the Order of the

[xii] Stauffer, V., The European Illuminati,

http://freemasonry.bcy.ca/anti-masonry/stauffer.html

Illuminati, with a membership of five all told. This organization would dissolve into nothing by 1790, but that has not stopped others from claiming to be the infamous Illuminati, and gaining fans and membership. There are no groups that exist today who are officially linked with this long-dissolved body, but that does not stop many from making the claims and money from their former existence.

There are anti-masonic crowd outcries that Masons sacrifice goats in their rituals. One such rant that is mostly commonly placed in public internet chat forums is the idea of riding a goat to become a Mason. From 2004 until 2009, I was a member of a clandestine Lodge and had never seen a goat or the sacrificing of a goat. I have been a regular Master Mason of the Grand Lodge of Illinois since 2010 and I have never seen a goat or rode a goat to become a member here as well. A longtime member of the clandestine lodge of which I was a member, told me once that the idea of a goat came about from Masons attempting to misdirect those who would seek to infiltrate a Masonic Lodge, in hopes that they if truly desired to become a member, they would be willing to "ride a goat."

In Albert Mackey's book, Encyclopedia *of Freemasonry* in 1873, he refers to Revered Dr. George Oliver's idea of the belief of why the profane believed Freemasons to be practicing some sort of witchcraft:

"Doctor Oliver says it was in England a common belief that the Freemasons were accustomed in their Lodges "to raise the Devil."[xiii] So the riding of the goat, which was believed to be practiced by the witches, was transferred to the Freemasons; and the saying remains to this day, although the belief has long since died out. To support the idea of my friend, it is conceivable that there would be some Masons who, out of fun or meaning to deter those only seeking membership out of curiosity, would be use this as a deterrent to keep them from petitioning.

Today, one can go to any Masonic store selling shirts or other Masonic paraphernalia, or any online internet Masonic store, and find items displaying pictures of Masons riding a goat. A simple Google search can produce images from the early 1900's of gentleman in tuxes, wearing Masonic aprons, riding goats. The Northern Light, a magazine for Masons of the Scottish rite, Northern Masonic Jurisdiction, has on its February 2011, Vol. 42, No. 1 issue a picture of a Bucking Billy Goat, made by the DeMoulin Brothers of Greenville, Illinois, made in the early 1900's. If one were not to read the article, they would assume it was used by Masons. It wasn't. It was used by the Odd Fellows, a fraternal group founded on the North American Continent in Baltimore, Maryland, on April 26, 1819 when

---

[xiii] Mackey, A. 1873, Encyclopedia of Freemasonry, Moss and co. pg. 800

"Thomas Wildey and four members of the Order from England instituted Washington Lodge No. 1."[xiv]

There have been Shriners in the past that have used a wooden goat to cart their newly initiated Nobles on, around the Temple, or where ever their creation, or the making of a Noble of the Mystic Shrine, took place. Lodges have even used them in play before or after an initiation to add levity to the experience until the early 1800's when the anti-Masonic movement took hold in the United States. They were removed from practice in any Lodge to promote the seriousness of Masonic work in the Lodge, and to separate it from the many fraternal groups that rose to popularity after the Great Depression.

[xiv] http://ioof.org/aboutus.html

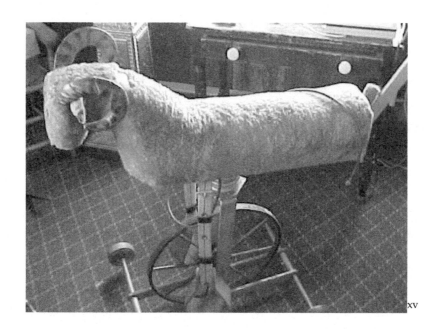

Another widely speculated theory is that the Masonic Fraternity is a religion. It is understood how the uninformed could reach a conclusion such as this. There is indeed scripture spoken in some parts of our ceremonies. The symbols depicting the two St. John's, the Baptist and the Evangelist, are used in Masonic symbolism. There is the use of an altar, a bible and a required professed of a belief in Deity to be admitted into our Lodges and partake of our rituals. So, it can be conceived by some that the Fraternity is a religion.

This is a huge misconception. Not only is the Fraternity of Freemasons not a religion, but the speaking of religion in a Lodge is forbidden. The Fraternity of Freemasons is a gentleman's Fraternity that is not even like a college Greek Fraternity. The very foundation of a Masonic Lodge is a secure place for the exchange of ideas, free from the influence of

xv http://www.phoenixmasonry.org/masonicmuseum/goat_riding_tricy

cle.htm

religion or politics, which can cause disharmony in the most welcomed circles. On many American Grand Lodge websites, there are sections giving attention to this question.

The Grand Lodge of California answers this question with the following:

"Is Masonry a religion?

Masonry is not a religion, nor is it a substitute for religion. The fraternity requires its members to have a belief in a Supreme Being and to belong to an established religion, but the fraternity itself is not affiliated with any religion, and men of all faiths are represented in the fraternity. Religion is not discussed at lodge meetings."[xvi]

[xvi] http://www.freemason.org/discoverMasonry/qa.htm#twelve

This misconception can be proven by different means. A look at the first known and accepted manuscript depicting the first rules and accepted behavior of Speculative Free-Masons, the *Regius Manuscript*, makes mention in line 684 that prayer should be done in Church.

"To telle mo medys of the masse:
To churche come [g]et, [g]ef thou may,
And here thy masse uche day;
[G]ef thou mowe not come to churche,
Wher that ever thou doste worche,
When thou herest to masse knylle,

Pray to God with herte stylle,
To [g]eve the part of that servyse,
That yn churche ther don yse."[xvii]

One can take a look at the first written *Masonic Constitution of 1723*, written by James Anderson, published once in 1723 and again in 1734.

"Therefore no private Piques or Quarrels must be brought within the Door of the Lodge, far less any Quarrels about Religion, or Nations, or State-Policy, we being only, as Masons, of the Catholick Religion above-mention'd ; we are also of all Nations, Tongues, Kindreds, and Languages, and are resolv'd against all Politicks, as what never yet conduc'd to the Welfare of the Lodge, nor ever will."[xviii]

[xvii] Regius Manuscript, on or about 1390

[xviii] Anderson, J. The Constitutions of the Free-Masons, 1734Pg. 53

Article 2

Notice that in the quote, it states the "Catholic Religion." Though Freemasonry is for all religions now, at its organization under the first Grand Lodge of England in 1717, it must be noted that Catholicism was the dominant religion in England in the 1700's. One could not have a legal society that excluded the Monarchy's religion if it were to have chance of staying in existence. This has changed in most countries, this policy of being Catholic, every country but Sweden, where once must profess a commitment to the Christian Faith to become a member.

In Albert Mackey's Compilation of the 25 Landmarks, he writes of the 21st:

"LANDMARK TWENTY-FIRST It is a Landmark, that a "Book of the Law" shall constitute an indispensable part of the furniture of every Lodge. I say advisedly, a Book of the Law, because it is not absolutely required that everywhere the Old and New Testaments shall be used. The "Book of the Law" is that volume which, by the religion of the country, is believed to contain the revealed will of the Grand Architect of the universe. Hence, in all Lodges in Christian countries, the Book of the Law is composed of the Old and New Testaments; in a country where Judaism was the prevailing faith, the Old Testament alone would be sufficient; and in Mohammedan countries, and among Mohammedan Masons the Koran might be substituted. Masonry does not attempt to interfere with the peculiar religious faith of its disciples, except so far as relates to the belief in the existence of God, and what necessarily results from that belief. The |"|Book of the Law|"| is to the speculative Mason his spiritual Trestle-board; without this he cannot labor; whatever he believes to be the revealed will of the Grand Architect constitutes for him this spiritual Trestle|-|board, and must ever be before him in his hours of speculative labor, to be the rule and guide of his conduct The Landmark, therefore, requires that a |"|Book of the Law,|"| a religious code of some kind, purporting to be an exemplar of the revealed will of God, shall form in essential part of the furniture of every Lodge."[xix]

It is important to note that while these all are noted as ancient usages of the Craft, the first a poem, the second, Ancient Charges of the Craft by James Anderson and the third, a revised and more comprehensive set of rules from Albert Mackey, these rules and landmarks though known universally, are not accepted universally. Each Masonic Grand Lodge has its own list of Craft Landmarks it chooses to enact into its Constitution and By-Laws. Every regular Grand Lodge has adopted if not all, at least some of the deemed important landmarks such as a required belief in Deity, a Grand Master presiding over the Grand Lodge with no authority over him, an obligation on the Volume of Sacred Law, or known as the Holy Book of an individual's faith, and other such notable landmarks that differentiate the Fraternity exclusively as Masonic and define a Lodge as a "regularly constituted lodge of Masons."

So, by the understanding of some of the distractions that Freemasons may face in the 21st century, more information must be now included in the education of a new Mason aside from the usual standard memorization and proficiency exam. Let us start with a purpose.

The purpose of the Fraternity has forever been attempted to be defined in one sentence, but is cannot be, because it serves various purposes to various men generating from many several different walks of life. The Grand Lodge of Illinois, to give a better summary of the purpose of the Fraternity has given the Craft a vision and mission statement: Fraternity, Enlightenment and Benevolence. These words give insight into ways the Fraternity seeks to inspire a man to become a better.

[xix] Anderson, J. The Constitutions of the Free-Masons, 1734Pg. 51

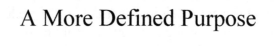
A More Defined Purpose

What drives us to seek to become better men? Or perhaps, what drives us to even seek how to become better men? This thought entered my mind as I participated in the ritual of a first degree in masonry one evening. As I conducted the candidate around the lodge, filling the chair of Senior Deacon and reciting the required ritual, I considered what might have motivated this good man to become a candidate for Freemasonry. What moved him to knock at the door of this Lodge for entrance?

Perhaps he witnessed a kind act of charity of a Shriner? He could have possibly heard of the great philosophy locked away in the Valley of the Scottish Rite. It could have even been the many stories told about the Knights Templar on the discovery channel and their connection to the King Solomon's treasure that caused rise to their curiosity. The reality is that it was more than likely a display of the tenets and practices of the usual customary behavior of a Mason, doing no more than exemplifying the behavior that the public has come to know that typifies an upright man that fancied this gentleman's interest in becoming a Mason. He was inspired to seek enlightenment.

Inspiration is a powerful emotion. It is, as Webster's Dictionary defines it, "the action or power of moving the intellect or emotions."[xx]   It causes feelings to stir to the point that a thought is formed or a physical movement is performed. When Veterans hear the Star-Spangled Banner played, and see the flag of the country wave, no matter how long they have been out of the service, their hearts beat a little stronger and their right hand is urged to move towards the top of their right eye brow and salute, it causes inspired thoughts, feelings and actions.

Hurricane Katrina brought destruction to the Gulf in August of 2009. The National Oceanic and Atmospheric

---

[xx] http://www.merriam-webster.com/dictionary/inspiration

Administration stated that "Katrina caused widespread devastation along the central Gulf Coast states of the US. Cities such as New Orleans, LA, Mobile, AL, and Gulfport, MS bore the brunt of Katrina's force and will need weeks and months of recovery efforts to restore normality."[xxi] As devastating as the winds blowing, and the massive amounts of water that came ashore in the storm surge was, it was not until the aftermath of the levees failing that people were truly crippled.

In the example of Hurricane Katrina, it is important to understand when people were inspired. It was not when the news broadcasters were battling to stand up against the head long winds. It was not when the politicians exclaimed how bad it was after the storm had passed that caused a nation to move. It was when the pictures were seen and voices were heard of people trapped on their roof tops that the agony of the situation caused emotions to stir into action. It was when a husband could share the horrendous moment he could not hold onto his wife's hand and had to watch her be swept away into the dark wetness of the night that people were inspired to answer the call of help. This is an example of how a negative situation causes positive inspiration.

It does not have to be the result of devastation and negativity that inspires one to desire to be, or to do better; it can also come from witnessing something small, simple, and positive. Each person has witnessed a small token of goodness during the holiday seasons. As we entered a shopping place of some sort and saw the salvation working shaking their bell, at one time or another, we have not really had the extra coin to give. Person after person walks by and maybe states that they will give on the way out of the store, but the charity worker has heard that line all day.

[xxi] http://www.ncdc.noaa.gov/special-reports/katrina.html

As you go to walk past the person shaking the bell, they catch eye contact with you. You thought for a quick second about how long this person has been standing in the cold ringing this bell and watching person after person give a holiday greeting and walk past, knowing just a couple of coins add up to a lot for charity organizations. You reach into your pocket and feel those two quarters that you were not going to use anyway, and before you know it, you have placed them in the donation basket.

"Thank you and God Bless you," the bell ringer states. Suddenly you get this warm glow all over and thought about how that was not really that hard. But what you may not have seen was the people behind you give immediately as well. They were not going too, but after you easily gave, they were inspired to as well. Witnessing your unselfish actions and hearing the warm response from the bell ringer caused an emotion to stir and a physical response to happen.

As Masons, our minds and consciousness should operate in the same manner, that we should be inspiring as well. We are given all these incredible tools and symbols that give us insight on how to behave. Squaring our actions, acting by the plumb, or parting upon the square, are the statements most commonly heard around a Lodge or explained at a Masonic function of sorts in front of the public. We are to constantly explore these meanings, and the countless others found within our lectures, and embark on discussions to speculate on how we can better implement them. One can smell a steak and imagine the taste of it. But, we can never truly understand the taste until we have eaten it. It then becomes part of us. We are then inspired to return later for more steak.

The application of Freemasonry is not something we simply do and repeat for it to become a part of our way of being. Open and close Lodge, discuss the bills and move candidates through the degrees, as if doing this is somehow practicing

Masonry. We are only repeating a learned behavior. Dogs do this every time they heard the wielding of a leash and the opening of the front door. It is simply operative learning. It is not Masonry.

It is the discussion and the absorption of it that truly changes a man. In the February 2012 Issue of the *Northern Light*, the Scottish rite magazine for the Northern Masonic Jurisdiction, Wayne T. Adams 33°, wrote an article by the name of *"Cornerstone of the Community."* This article conveyed how Freemasonry was woven into the fabric of every city as new world, the United States, expanded in population and spread from the east coast into the west. While explaining, what was so magnetic in the Craft then, in the 18th and 19th Century, he explained very bluntly what was practiced then, versus now.

Brother Adams explained, "The second part – the lectures – contain words and phrases which are drawn from the philosophy of the Enlightenment, a philosophy which is outward looking, which teaches the brotherhood and equality of all men; toleration and respect for all men of good will; the need to live in a world marked by harmony and cooperation; the importance of public service, and striving to improve."[xxii] The first half of our degrees is only a re-enactment of the operative Mason guilds and their initiations, opening and closings. Brethren have forgotten that the second half of our ritual is the speculative portion of our studies.

This begs the question: If we are not treating the second half of our ritual as importantly as we treat the first half, then what are we discussing in our lodges in the way of Masonic knowledge for Brethren to eat and digest? What part of the learning of Masonry are we absorbing to make it apart of ourselves? And, if we are not discussing the absorbent amount

[xxii] http://supremecouncil.org/rss/February2012/201202-04.htm

of speculative knowledge that gives us extracts from the Egyptians, to the Mayans to the great Greek philosophers, what are displaying that resembles the Freemasonry our forefathers left us to practice? How are we to masonically inspire?

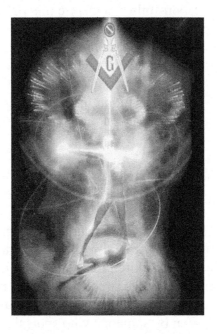

So, as I walked this candidate through the first degree, I continued to think to myself, "I wonder if he will find the same inspiration that brought him here, to keep him here." I wondered even more as the lectures of the second half of the ritual were explained without enthusiasm, "I wonder if the candidate is being inspired?" I know I am inspired, but I already know the lectures, I have read them and analyzed them. I also only have had a few Brethren as excited as I was to study and explore the ritual. Most times, I had to look to Brethren further away from my home as I would have liked to find some of the understanding I sought.

My question became, how will this new Brother be inspired enough to seek out beyond the confines of this one

Lodge, to seek the knowledge he was initially inspired to come here to acquire? Will he absorb enough to improve the way he thinks and acts to inspire another to seek? This means that a more experienced Brother that knows what it will take must shoulder the responsibility to inspire this Brother, in hopes that it will be reciprocated to another along the way. One Brother asked another once how he could repay him for the insight he had given him. He stated, "Teach someone else and share with them what I have shared with you." It was almost a verbal example of a Chain of Union. Inspiration must be created and then exchanged in a never-ending cycle of one brother inspiring another.

As the knowledge of Freemasonry could fill an abyss, the search for inspiration is only as far away as a book, a discussion, an examination of philosophy. It is also as closely found in witnessing the gift of helping handicapped children by the Shriners, or the charity found within the contributions by the Scottish Rite for its children Learning Centers, or even the Knights Templar Eye Research foundation. But most of all, inspiration is found in the actions of each individual Mason, unknowingly seen by someone who spots the Masonic emblem on his ring and watches how he interacts with his spouse or his children, how he settles confrontations amongst co-workers, the responsible way he conducts business when the supervisor is not around, or how he simply just "IS." Each one of us is the Masonic inspiration for someone else.

The Masonic institution is very complex. For centuries, it has endured distractions along the way. There will always be differences in ideas of how Freemasonry is to be practiced and still be considered regular in its function. There were the differences between the Premier Grand Lodge of England formed in 1717, and the self-designated Ancient Grand Lodge of England formed in 1751, which ended in 1813 when the two Grand Lodges uniting, the former having been operating to appease the aristocracy of England. These Grand Lodges have since united into the United Grand Lodge of England. There was the anti-Masonic period of the early 1800's that resulted in the abandonment of many Lodges in the United States. There was also the removal of a profession of Deity for a candidate's initiation into the jurisdiction of the Grand Orient of France, making them an irregular Grand Lodge. And we come to the clandestine Lodges that exist in the United States and England. The institution has continued to make good men better through the ages.

[xxiii]

[xxiii] www.livingstonesmagazine.com advertisement

Chapter 2

The Origins of the Fraternity of Freemasons

The Commonly Accepted History

There are many speculative beliefs as to the origin of Freemasonry. If one performs a search on the internet or perhaps participate in social groups located on different web pages, they may come across conversations that originate from different beginnings, all of which they attempt to prove without any doubt, "the source." What must be done is to first separate the beginnings of organized Fraternity from the source of the philosophic messages located within the lectures and ritual. The organizing of the Fraternity in its structure, and the collection of knowledge found within the rituals of Freemasonry, existing as a repository for this knowledge, are two distinct differences and require to distinct explanations. The following is a brief, but illustrated explanation, of the common and proven accepted beginnings of the organization of the formation of the Fraternity of speculative Freemasons.

The organized Fraternity of Freemasons has its origins within the stone mason guilds of Great Britain, prior to the age of Enlightenment of the 18th century. Kevin L. Gest, author of *The Secrets of Solomon's Temple* and *Chivalry*, makes note of a quote in his latest book, *The Mandorla and Tau*: from *The Story of the City Companies* by P.H. Ditchfield MA FSA quoting King Edward III, "There was much riot and disturbance in London at this period, and the Gilds as secret societies, were regarded with some ill-favour by the authorities, and as an element of danger."[xxiv] The end of these negative aspersions was the granting of incorporation of the Sovereign. So, even before the establishment of the Premier Grand Lodge in London, England in 1717, and before the *Regius Manuscript* of 1390, the idea of

---

[xxiv] Gest, K. 2011, The Mandorla and Tau, Lewis Masonic, pg. 79 The

quote is from the book The Story of the City

Companies by P.H. Ditchfield MA FSA, and he is quoting Edward III

monarch 1327-1377

the existence of these guilds with membership already deemed to be exclusive, garnered criticism from the public of their "secret" activities.

One must note that these merchant guilds, as they were in London before the stone masons, originally began as religious guilds with benefits available to the members, comprising of fellowshipping in the same manner Freemasons and other fraternal groups do today. They partook in meals, toasts and conversation, beginning three decades or so after Charles II's death. The transition of guilds from religious to social would occur when Henry VIII created the Church of England.[xxv]

The merchant and trade gilds existed in the same manner as trade unions today. They regulated who would be admitted, identifying who were qualified to do the work or not. They also regulated the work they would do. These stone gilds were

[xxv] http://www.mastermason.com/wnymasons/

Silver_Lodge/History/History%20of%20Freemasonry_files/cantiere02.

Jpg

governed by a "Court of Assistants, which comprises a Master, who is elected and two Wardens, with the earliest records of an organization for the regulation of the Craft of Stonemasonry being 1356."[xxvi] After the Black Plague ravaged Europe and ended, and the public smilingly had enough with the privileged class of workman of the merchant gilds, the system dissolved. The stone gilds would not flourish, but still exist until eventually evolving into trade unions.

The religious gilds would transition into social societies instead of disappearing altogether though. The social guilds would become the true first benefit societies, like the "golden age of fraternalism," described in *American Freemasons* by Mark A. Tabbert. "Between 1865 and 1900, more than 235 fraternal orders were founded (16 in 1896 alone) with as many as six million members."[xxvii] Still, like the age of the fraternal boom in America, these early gilds would not be Masonic in nature, as in having a specific purpose of ritual to improve the spiritual and philosophical needs of man, but strictly social benefit societies to protect certain groups and aid financially for burial members and such needs.

It would not be until the finding of the *Regius Manuscript*, believed to be written about 1390, was found to be a Masonic document by Mr. James Orchard Halliwell-Philips and in it contained the written connection in poem form between freemasonry and the stone masons. The insight into the birth of speculative masonry being practiced within a stone mason's gild

[xxvi] Gest, K. 2011, The Mandorla and Tau, Lewis Masonic, pg. 79 The

quote is from the book The Story of the City

[xxvii] Tabbert, M. 2005, American Freemason: Three Centuries of Building

Communities, New York University Press;

Alvin J. Schmidt, 1980, Fraternal Organizations, Greenwood Press

would be explained. Mr. Halliwell-Philips was a Shakespearean scholar and literary collector who lived between the year 1820 and 1889. "In 1872 and subsequent years James Orchard Halliwell (he added the maiden name of his wife Henrietta, daughter of the antiquary and collector Sir Thomas Phillips, in 1872) presented to the University Library ca 1,000 printed volumes on Shakespeare together with 100 volumes of notebooks and diaries as well as 300 volumes of literary correspondence."[xxviii]

The manuscript gives insight into how each mason regarded one another as brothers, rather than an apprentice or a master of the trade. This is used as a term of endearment amongst the members.

> "But masons should never one another call,
> Within the craft amongst them all,
> Neither subject nor servant, my dear brother,
> Though he be not so perfect as is another;
> Each shall call other fellows by friendship."[xxix]

Here we see the reference that all masons are to be equals, being "neither subject nor servant, my dear brother." Freemasons have an expression that we "Meet each other on the level."

This expression symbolizes that neither rank nor wealth obtained in society amongst the profane gave any Mason a title of such over another within the confines of a Lodge, or amongst its members. Egos from titles gained in society have no place in a Masonic lodge. The reason for this is that it prevents a free

---

[xxviii] http://www.docs.is.ed.ac.uk/docs/libarchive/

bgallery/Gallery/records/eighteen/halliwell.html

[xxix] Regius Manuscript, 1390 appox.

exchange of ideas. All regular Masons are equal amongst the Fraternity.

Another word to point out is that of a Fellow, noting, "Each shall call other fellows by friendship." Before the 1500's, there were only two titles amongst men of the Craft, that of Master of the Lodge and Fellows of the Craft. Only the Fellow who demonstrated the most knowledge and leadership was elected to the office of master of the craft. This idea of the most experienced, or the one who exemplified the merit worthy of the responsibility to teach the Craft from the symbolic position of wisdom, would find its way into the constitutions written by James Anderson in 1734.

> "All Preferment among Masons is grounded upon real
> Worth and personal Merit only; that so the Lords may be
> Well served, the Brethren not put to Shame, nor the Royal
> Craft despis'd: Therefore no Master or Warden is chosen
> By Seniority, but for his Merit. It is impossible to describe
> These things in writing, and every Brother must attend in his
> Place, and learn them in a way peculiar to this Fraternity:
> Only Candidates may know, that no Master should take an
> Apprentice, unless he has sufficient Imployment for him,
> And unless he be a perfect Youth, having no Maim or Defect
> In his Body, that may render him uncapable of learning
> The Art, of serving his Master's LORD, and of being made a
> Brother, and then a Fellow-Craft in due time, even after he
> Has served such a Term of Years as the Custom of the Country
> Directs; and that he should be descended of honest Parents; That
> so, when otherwise qualify'd, he may arrive to the Honour of
> being the WARDEN, and then the Master of
> The Lodge, the Grand Warden, and at length the
> GRANDMASTER
> Of all the Lodges, according to his Merit."[xxx]

[xxx] Anderson, J. 1834, The Constitutions of Free-Masons, London, pgs

"The most expert of the Fellow-Craftsmen shall be chosen
Or appointed the Master, or Overseer of the Lord's Work;
Who is to be call'd MASTER by those that work under him."[xxxi]

Other manuscripts that were found to demonstrate a creation of the speculative Freemason from the operative Masons consist of:

- Halliwell Manuscript - Supposed - 1390
  Housed in the King's Library, British Museum
- Cooke Manuscript - Supposed 1490
- Dowland Manuscript - Supposed 1500
- Landsdowne Manuscript - Supposed 1560
- York Manuscript, No. 1 - Supposed 1600
- Harleian Manuscript, No. 2054 - Supposed 1625
  Housed in the Archives of the Grand Lodge of England
- Grand Lodge Manuscript - Supposed 1583
  Housed in the Archives of the Grand Lodge of England.
- Sloane Manuscript, No. 3848 - Certain 1646
  Housed in the British Museum
- Sloane Manuscript, No. 3323 - Certain 1659-
- Harleian Manuscript, No. 1942 - Supposed 1660
- Aitcheson-Haven Manuscript - Supposed 1666
  Housed in the Grand Lodge of Scotland
- Edinburgh-Kilwinning Manuscript - Supposed 1670
  Housed in the Mother Lodge Kilwinning, No. 0, Scotland
- York Manuscript, No. 5 - Supposed 1670
- York Manuscript, No. 6 - Supposed 1670
- Lodge of Antiquity Manuscript - Certain 1686
- York Manuscript, No. 2 - Certain 1693
- Alnwick Manuscript - Certain 1701
  In possession of the Newcastle College of Rosicrucians

50, 51

[xxxi] Anderson, J. pg 51

- York Manuscript No. 4 - Certain 1704
- Papworth Manuscript - Supposed 1714

Manuscripts that have been collected over time are extremely important to the Craft. From the *Regius Manuscript* of 1390 to the latest, the *Papworth Manuscript* of 1714, these are important because they establish what is referred to as the "Ancient Charges." These charges demonstrate the development of the Craft from operative to speculative. They show the additions of information found with the lectures of the Craft.

Though manuscripts illustrate a progressive mindset towards a speculative craft from an operative one, there are no Lodge minutes contained within these documents. Lodge minutes are a written as a record of transactions of a meeting. These minutes are what can be referenced to give a depiction of what transpired in a meeting at a certain time in history. In the Lodge of Edinburgh, located in Scotland, there still exist minutes of an occurrence that would mark an official change in practice of the initiating of men into a stonemason's Lodge for other reasons than making them an apprentice of a stone mason for trade work.

The Minutes of Edinburgh Lodge, dating back to 1599, record that Robert Moray, "described as Quartermaster to the Army of Scotland, then on English soil, had been made a Mason at Newcastle, May 20, 1641, and the Minute thus made was for authenticating and registering his membership in the Lodge."[xxxii] This would mark a clear indication of a change in the practice of operative stone masons' lodges. But, why and what would make these stone masons, master builders, accept a man into their gild?

By the beginning of the 17th century, the need for monumental cathedrals waned and the membership of the stone

---

[xxxii] http://encyclopediaoffreemasonry.com/m/moray-sir-robert/

gilds were in great decline. Some historians suggest that to keep the gilds alive, men were initiated into them, thus making it a social gild rather than a trade's gild. The great fire in London in 1666, occurring just 12 months after the Great Plague, would prove to be the last hurrah of the trade. During the reign of King Charles II. A fire would break out in the city made of wood, and give a chance for much needed stone work for Masons.

"The fire started in Pudding Lane. The fire started in a baker's shop owned by Thomas Farriner – who was the king's baker, his maid failed to put out the ovens at the end of the night. The heat created by the ovens caused sparks to ignite the wooden home of Farriner. In her panic, the maid tried to climb out of the building but failed. She was one of the few victims of the fire. Once it started, the fire spread quickly. The city was basically made from wood and with September following on from the summer, the city was very dry. Strong winds fanned the flames."[xxxiii]

Operative Masons from all over Great Britain would converge on the work made available. King Charles II would see to protect the tradesman of his empire, granting Royal Charters to the Lodges of London and West Minster, that prevented Masons from other areas of Great Britain from moving in and hoarding the work. To understand exactly how much work was to be protected, William Preston writes in his book, *Illustrations of Masonry*, "Jonas Moore and Ralph Gatrix, who were appointed surveyors on this occasion to examine the ruins, reported that the fire over-ran 373 acres within the walls, and burnt 13,000 houses, 89 parish churches, besides chapels, leaving only 11 parishes standing."[xxxiv]

[xxxiii] http://www.historylearningsite.co.uk/great_fire_of_london_of_1666.h

tm

[xxxiv] William Preston, 1867, 2012, Illustrations of Masonry, this book was

Though the fire would give a last rush of work for the operative masons, the decline of work prior to the fire would continue to spurn the growth of initiated gentleman into the Craft for speculative purposes. The lodges were a mixed membership consisting of both operative and speculative masons. The growth in membership of purely speculative masons was not substantial. It would not be until after 1702 that the old Lodge of St. Paul and other lodges that meet regularly, would make a proposal and an agreement would be officially made that, "The privileges of Masonry should no longer be restricted to operative masons, but extend to men of various professions, provided they were regularly approved and initiated into the order."[xxxv]

---

originally written in 1776, two years after

Preston was Master of the Lodge of Antiquity. Pg. 136

[xxxv] Preston, illustrations of Masonry, pg. 149

A Grand Lodge is formed in England

It is commonly accepted that there were four Lodges that met to form what would become the first, or premier, speculative Masonic Grand Lodge in the world. The Goose and Gridiron Ale-house, the Crown Ale-house, the Apple-Tree Tavern and the Rummer and Grapes Tavern, all met at the Apple-tree Tavern to create this Grand Lodge. The oldest Master Mason, Anthony Sayer, was elected the first Grand Master. Captain Joseph Elliot and Jacob Lamball, a carpenter, were elected the Grand Wardens.

There was no large edifice for these Masons of the first Grand Lodge to meet in. The Grand Lodge existed were ever these men would decide to hold their quarterly meetings. As is indicated by the names of the first places these lodges met, the lodges that organized the first grand lodge were in taverns.

From this formation in 1717 of the world's first speculative Masonic Grand Lodge, with a jurisdiction extending just seven miles from its establishment in London, England, to the almost 100 Regular Grand Lodges in the United States, and a regularly formed Grand Lodge in almost every country that practices democracy around the globe, it was quite a laudable undertaking that the men may not have even realized they were creating.

There is a common thought that this Grand Lodge, recognized to be the first legitimate operative Masonic Grand Lodge in world, is the authority of all Grand Lodges in the world. This is simply not true. It does not grant charters to other Grand Lodges, nor does it interfere with the decisions of any other Grand Lodge in the world. On the website of the United Grand lodge of England, it specifically states exactly the territory it governs stating, "The United Grand Lodge of England (UGLE) is the governing body of Freemasonry in England, Wales and the Channel Islands. Its headquarters are at Freemasons' Hall, Great Queen Street, London WC2B 5AZ."[xxxvi]

It is held in the Ancient Usages of Freemasonry that all Masonic Grand Lodges are sovereign and are forbidden with interfering in the affairs of another. This is exemplified today as in the United States, there exists a separation of predominately black membership and predominately white membership in Grand Lodges. The Grand Lodges with predominately black membership are known as Prince Hall Affiliated Grand Lodges and the Grand Lodges with predominately white membership are those that have existed first in their territory, where no other Grand Lodge was previously formed in what is referred to as conforming to the ancient usages and in regular practice- the Exclusive Territorial Doctrine.

The Prince Hall Affiliated Grand Lodges, which were considered irregularly formed, even though the nature of their original forming is now accepted by the United Grand Lodge of England, were not recognized for hundreds of years as being legitimate Masonic Grand Lodges. The United Grand Lodge of England originally contended that they could not intervene in the recognition of the Most Worshipful Prince Hall Grand Lodge of Massachusetts by their Grand Lodge because there already existed a Massachusetts Grand Lodge they had established a recognition compact agreement.

Prince Hall, whom the original African Grand Lodge was renamed in honor of, "was born on September 12, 1748 at Bridgetown, Barbados, British West Indies [so it is thought]. His father, Thomas Prince Hall, was an Englishman and his mother of French descent. He was apprenticed as a leather worker---- came to the United States in 1765 at the age of 17-applied himself industriously to common labor during the day and studied privately at night. Upon reaching the age of 27, he had acquired the fundamentals of an education. Saving his earnings,

---

xxxvi http://www.ugle.org.uk/about-ugle/

he had accumulated sufficient funds to buy a piece of property. He joined the Methodist Church in which he passed as an eloquent preacher. His first church was in Cambridge, Massachusetts."[xxxvii]

On April 9, 1770, Prince Hall, who was born into slavery, received his Certificate of Manumission. It stated:

"This may certify it may concern that Prince Hall has lived with us 21 (date unclear - may be 25) years and has served us well upon all occasions for which reason we maturely give him his freedom and he is no longer Reckoned a slave but has always accounted as a freeman by us as he has served us faithfully upon that account we have given him his freedom as witness our hands this ninth day of April 1770."[xxxviii] Thus, making Prince Hall a free man.

He and 14 other men were raised to the sublime degree of master mason in Lodge no. 441 in 1775 in Boston, Massachusetts. Lodge no. 441, a Lodge under the jurisdiction of the Grand Lodge of Ireland, held in the 38th Foot, was present in New York City at the formulating of the Grand Lodge of New York in June 1781."[xxxix]

[xxxvii] Records in the custody of the Grand Lodge of Ireland are the following: -

Transcript of Minutes covering the period 1796 to 1821.

Original in the care of the Officers' Mess, 1st Btn. South Staffordshire Regt.

[xxxviii] http://www.conferenceofgrandmasterspha.org/gmasters_history.asp

[xxxix] http://www.conferenceofgrandmasterspha.org/gmasters_history.asp

There are common misconceptions about Prince Hall Masonry and its reasons for not being recognized as a regular Masonic jurisdiction by the nine former confederate states of the southern United States. One is that these states do not desire to recognize Prince Hall Masonry because of racism against black people. While there are instances of racism in all parts of our country, there are both truths and untruths surrounding this issue, which we will delve into further into this book.

One aspect of the speculation of Prince Hall Masonry held in the clandestine Masonic community is that Freemasonry was derived from Egypt and being such, the black man owns it and should not ask the white man for permission to practice it. Another widely held statement among clandestine masons is that because Prince Hall is not recognized by nine of the southern states, it authorizes any group to start a black masonic lodge, attempting to justify their existence because of the situation that exists in the south. This is the mindset that, "If they are not recognizing you as Masons anyway, it does not matter if we are recognized either." This is a fallacy to justify the imitation of such an honorable fraternity and all making such claims need to be consistently educated with credible facts for further research. Let us look at the different claims of the origin of the Fraternity of speculative Freemasons.

First, we will look at the claim of the Egyptian origin. One claim of Egyptian Masonry is the Egyptian Rite, created by Count Cagliostro. In the book, *Cagliostro and his Egyptian Rite of Freemasonry*, by Henry R. Evans, Cagliostro, the "rosicrucian and archnecromancer of the eighteenth century, who suddenly emerged from profound obscurity, flashed like a meteor across the stage of life, and then vanished in darkness in the gloomy dungeons of the castle of San Leon, Italy, charged by the Church of Rome with magic, heresy, and Freemasonry..."[xl] He did

---

[xl] Evans, H., 2003, Cagliostro and his Egyptian Rite of Freemasonry, A

actually exist, and founded the Egyptian Rite, patterning it after Freemasonry, as he was a Freemason himself.

It is not known what happened to Cagliostro as he spent time in the dungeons of the Italian jail, but it is believed that he may have developed a split personality, or something of the sort, as he did possess magical powers, or what we today would refer to as extra sensory perception. Known as a conman before his imprisonment, when he abilities did not produce at demand, he would resort to slight-of-hand tricks that caused some to speculate if in fact he was magical, or was he simply a great conman that got caught making magic up from time to time. Research has been done on the history of Count Cagliostro by Philippa Faulks and Robert L.D. Cooper in the book, *The Magic Magician*.

The Ancient and Primitive Rite of Memphis Misraim, a supposed operative craft system not associated with regular Freemasonry in the United States, composed of 99°, is claimed by the Grand Orient Egyptian Official Formation of Masonieria Egipcia del Antiguo Primitivo Rito de Memphis Misraim M.E.A.P.R.M.M. USA, to be a direct descendant of the Cagliostro Egyptian Rite. While there is a manuscript ritual of the Egyptian Ritual in possession by the Grand Lodge of Scotland, there is no definitive linkage to connect the Ancient and Primitive Rite of Memphis Misraim with the Egyptian Rite of Cagliostro. So, while the ritual does exist, it is not recognized as standard ritual to be practiced in the mainstream masonic society of the United States. It does not adhere to the ancient landmarks by admitting woman, and does not have sovereign Grand Lodges, and therefore cannot even be considered for recognition.

Master of Magic, Pg. 1, Cornerstone Book

Publishers Lafayette, LA

From the Egyptian Rite, we turn to the Moorish Rite of Freemasonry. This clandestine Masonry is founded on the belief that Freemasonry came directly from the Moors making claims such as, "Few realize that Freemasonry was practiced in Meso-America by indigenous people (Moors) in their socio-religious systems."[xli] While Freemasonry in the speculative sense has its origins in symbolism from Egypt and other early societies, it also derives its philosophical influence from western philosophy, eastern philosophy, and many other early mystery initiatic systems.

It is these pseudo-masonic organizations that call for attention to the known facts of the establishment of the premier Grand Lodge of England in 1717. The speculative nature of the philosophical context of ritual, while derived from the many mystery schools that have existed from time immemorial, it is beyond contestation the formation of the world's first speculative Masonic Grand Lodge.

The negative effects of pseudo-masonic organizations such as this and others, notably the International Modern Free and Accepted Masons, the Modern Free and Accepted Masons, and many other smaller organizations that seek to be recognized as Scottish rite organizations, they all prey on the miss-informed man seeking to become a true Freemason. As it is explained further in the book, these organizations exist without any masonic authority. Masonic authority is derived from the ancient usages and standards of Freemasonry, which regard legitimacy of origin as one of the three principle factors in determining legitimacy.

Any man, seeking to become a Freemason, sees men who regard themselves as Masons wearing jackets and hats displaying themselves as such, and he assumes he is approaching the

---

[xli] http://www.moorishriteonline.net/freemasonry.htm

appropriate people to enter the fraternity. The biggest problem is not of their existence, but of their disclosure to potential candidates.

Many of these organizations have website that explain their history, starting with the Grand Lodge of England, which may seem to legitimize them, but it is simply false advertising. This is an account of the history of the International Free and Accepted Modern Masons, Inc., taken from their website:

"International Free & Accepted Modern Masons, Inc. and Order of Eastern Star is a worldwide fraternity organized in 1950 by the late Dr. William V. Banks, a very prominent Attorney and a Mason with very high ideals. We received our charter in 1950. Dr. Banks dream became a reality with the birth of this new Masonic Organization. Our purpose is to provide moral, financial, benevolent, and charitable leadership to serve this present age."[xlii]

Dr. William V. Banks, Founder
WGPR-TV - Channel 62 - 1975
Detroit [xliii]

[xlii] http://internationalmasons.org/about_us.html

[xliii] http://internationalmasons.org/about_us.html

"The institution of Free and Accepted Masonry is the outgrowth of Ancient Free Masonry, as adopted by Modern Masons in 1717 at the Apple Tree Tavern, England. It adheres to the ancient moral principles of Freemasonry, but has been modified from time to time, that it may have all current and modern benefits to be offered by a Free Mason Fraternal Order. We have no quarrels with other Masonic Bodies, and will be glad to cooperate with them in building Masonry as a True Righteous Order based on the principles of the Holy Bible."[xliv]

"Having been incorporated and chartered in August of 1950; our Charter empowered International Masons to practice Freemasonry, and operate as a Masonic Order, throughout the United States, its possessions and territories. This American issued charter empowers International Masons to the same rights as those charters issued directly from the Grand Lodge of England or the Grand Orient of France. Dr. Banks and his host of friends established a National Jurisdiction. Through their diligent efforts, the same year, three States were incorporated: Ohio, New York and Illinois."[xlv]

As can be clearly seen by the second paragraph explanation of their history, they claim they have their origin as an "outgrowth" of Freemasonry having begun in Apple Tree Tavern, they state Freemasonry has, "modified from time to time, that it may have all current and modern benefits to be offered by a Free Mason." In this statement, they allude that they provide to one of the rights and privileges of a Master Mason, being that this includes the right to visit and sit with other regular and accepted Masons, but this is not true. Of the more than 2 million Masons in the United States alone, Clandestine Masons of this organization cannot visit or speak masonically with any of them. Because this groups are

[xliv] http://internationalmasons.org/about_us.html

[xlv] http://internationalmasons.org/about_us.html

clandestine due to origin and structure, they could never be considered for recognition by any regular Masonic Grand Lodge in the world.

Further manipulation occurs when members are confronted as to their claim of their members can visit regular Lodges. One member stated, "We are free to visit any lodge, it is the white and Prince Hall Lodges that do not respect the right of a Master Mason to visit and sit in Lodge together." So, it is believed that the ownness of the inability to visit regular lodges is the fault of the rules of the regular lodges, and not theirs. Prince Hall Affiliated Masonry is regular and has been accepted as such due to the possession of the original charter issued to Prince Hall.

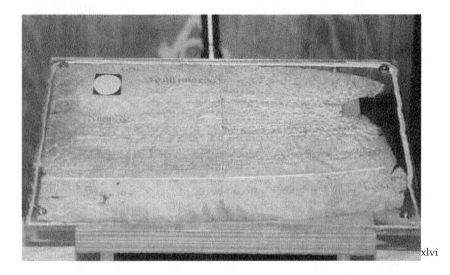

xlvi

When I found out that the Lodge I had membership in was not chartered by a Grand Lodge that would not under any circumstances allow me to travel and speak further about Freemasonry, I was to say the least very upset. I had spent countless hours in the contribution of my time, a lot of money,

xlvi http://www.thephylaxis.org/phylaxis/index.php

and developed friendships based on the premise that what I had become a member of was part of the world-wide fraternity of freemasons. This feeling is duplicated all the time by men finding out their severe limitation at the exercising of their rights and privileges as master masons, and this is one of the first negative effects of the existence in the United States, and other countries, of organizations not masonically authorized to exist as the representation of the Fraternity.

Another tangible negative effect is membership in the Fraternity. Documentation of the amount of men who are members of these organizations are not known as they are clandestine and do not report to regular masonic grand lodges. However, per the Phylaxis society, there are more than 57 clandestine Grand Lodge in the state of Illinois alone.[xlvii] Consider that number for a moment. One state, 57 unauthorized Grand Lodges existing, all competing for membership, and though this affects the Grand Lodge of Illinois in potential members, the Most Worshipful Prince Hall Grand Lodge, with approximately over 4000 members in the entire state, are at a greater disadvantage for gaining potential new members.

I attended a car show on the south side of Chicago one year. I had on a baseball cap with the masonic square and compass engraved on the front. Within a couple minutes of being at the event, I had already been approached by several men stating they were Masons. They showed in public the first-degree penalty. Upon asking them what Grand Lodge they held membership in, not one was a regular Grand Lodge. Consider the possibility as how many times a day this occurrence happens to how many more Masons? It is quite an epidemic in the larger cities of the United States.

[xlvii] http://www.thephylaxis.org/phylaxis/index.php

What are the larger ramifications of these clandestine Masons, predominately black and in the larger cities, to the rest of the Masonic world? There is the negative effect on Masons who have negative racial residual feelings from generational separatism of the races that justify their position that only whites should be in one lodge and only blacks should be in their own lodge. One Mason speaking on a public internet forum stated, "Blacks have their own lodges, we have our own lodges. We don't mix because that is how 'they' act." I purposely withhold the name of the gentleman, but I will note that these remarks were from a Mason in Texas, whose Grand Lodge has amity with the Most Worshipful Prince Hall Grand Lodge of Texas. Even with fraternal relations established, it is evident that some still will view Freemasonry practiced better with a "separate but equal" mindset. Can it be conceivable that these feelings truly exist within the Fraternity? And if they do in fact exist, the behavior of men claiming to be Masons, with behavior that suffers no consequence of expulsion from the fraternity, is left unregulated and negatively influencing men that affect potential fellowshipping with regular Masons they have never even met.

Racism in the Fraternity? That is covered later in the book.

What can be done to stop the bleeding of this unimaginable negative activities of unregulated Masons? Some would suggest that we do not worry about it. Do nothing, they say. We only want good men and if a man does not realize he is a part of a clandestine Lodge than that is his fault. When he wants to become a real mason, he will come and find us. Is this a realistic option? It happens occasionally, a man finds out by accident that he is a member of a clandestine lodge, but if no one told him, would he ever know? What happens when the activity of this clandestine membership displays activities that are contrary to being upright and moral, such as paddling candidates during initiations, shooting them with water guns, or other more sinister forms of hazing? The gentleman quits, thinking that Freemasonry is about beating others, and a potentially very good man walks away believing something that is a lie, and he repeats this occurrence to everybody he can tell to prevent others from joining. Do you think this doesn't happen? It does. I was paddled in the clandestine Lodge to which I belonged.

There are laws in several states against the impersonation of a Freemason. New York Law, "N.Y. GBS. LAW § 137 : NY Code - Section 137: Unauthorized wearing or use of badge, name or insignia of certain orders and societies, states, "Any person who wilfully wears, or attaches to any motor vehicle, the badge, insignia, rosette or the button of the…insignia or emblem of any lodge, society or organization subordinate to or recognized as Masonic by the Grand Lodge of Free and Accepted Masons of the State of New York, or the insignia or emblem of the Masonic War Veterans of the State of New York, Inc., or the insignia or emblem of the Order of the Eastern Star of the State of New York…"[xlviii]

[xlviii] http://www.thephylaxis.org/phylaxis/index.php

CONNECTICUT FREEMASONS

GRAND LODGE of ANCIENT FREE & ACCEPTED MASONS
of the STATE of CONNECTICUT

ROBERT G. FITZGERALD
GRAND SECRETARY
PO Box 250
Wallingford, CT 06492

BUSINESS PHONE
(203) 679-5903
FAX NUMBER
(203) 679-5996
grandlodge@masonicare.org

March 1, 2007

Purpose: To update Section 6206 language to make it agree with the Connecticut General Statute cited. Present wording:

Section 6206. Extract From General Statutes of State Re: Unlawful Wearing of Insignia. By statute law of Connecticut (Section 53-377, General Statutes, 1958, as amended), it is a penal offense, punishable with a fine of not more than five hundred dollars ($500), to willfully wear the insignia, rosette or badge of any fraternal order, or use the same to obtain aid or assistance, or to use the name of any such society, organization or order, or the titles of its officers, or its ritual or ceremonies, unless entitled to do so under the Constitution, By-laws or Rules and Regulations of such order or society, or to claim to be a member thereof, with intent to deceive or defraud. This applies to clandestine lodges, clandestinely made Masons or imposters whose acts come within the statute adopted.

Actual Connecticut Statute wording with applicable portion in underlined italics:

Sec. 53-377. *Fraudulent uses of badges or insignia. Any person who copies, imitates or simulates* the

---

The photograph of the Connecticut General Statute cites:

Purpose: To update Section 6206 language to make it agree with the Connecticut General Statute cited. Present wording:

Section 6206. Extract from General Statutes of State Re: Unlawful Wearing of Insignia. By statute law of Connecticut (Section 53-377, General Statutes, 1958, as amended), it is penal offense, punishable with a fine of not more than five hundred dollars ($500), to willfully wear the insignia, rosette or badge of any fraternal order, or use the same to obtain aid or assistance, or to use the name of any such society, organization or order, or the titles of its officers, or its ritual or ceremonies, unless entitled to do so under the Constitution, By-laws or Rules and Regulations of such order or society, or to claim to be a member thereof, with intent to deceive or defraud. This applies to clandestine lodges, clandestinely made masons or imposters whose acts come within the statute adopted.

Several Prince Hall Grand Lodges have taken Clandestine Grand Lodges to court in both Georgia and Pennsylvania, such as the International Free and Modern Masons, most recognizable with a key affixed to the square and compass, gaining a judgment in the case to have these organizations "no longer practice the rituals of Freemasonry, present themselves as Masons, wear any regalia representing themselves as Masons, or having the word Freemason even in the name of their organization."[xlix]

The answer is not to have new laws created, but to enforce laws that already exist. Clandestine Masons have existed since the time of the mid-1730's, including the Grand Lodge known as the "Ancients," formed in 1756 that eventually united with the premier Grand Lodge of England in 1717, and formed the now United Grand Lodge of England. So, they have existed for a long time in the past, they exist in absorbent amounts today, and perhaps will exist long into the future. There is no way to make them become non-extinct, but they can be limited.

[xlix] http://www.thephylaxis.org/phylaxis/index.php

In has been speculated by some that the square and compass emblem, the most visible sign of Freemasonry, cannot be trademarked. This is incorrect. There are Grand Lodges that have placed copyrights on the symbol. In 1992 the Grand Lodge of Pennsylvania registered the square and compasses for their jurisdiction and the Masonic Service Association of North America sent a letter to all U.S. Grand Secretaries explaining that, "As there is no U.S. masonic national authority, each Grand Lodge would have to register independently. Although Pennsylvania offered to assist other jurisdictions if they so desired, the MSA does not know how many have since registered."[1]

Per the Grand Lodge of Michigan Constitutions and By-Laws, "Art. XXXI, 4-31 Sec. 2, any non-mason that uses the names and emblems (square and compasses) can be taken to court under the Michigan Annotated Statutes 18.641-18.647, 18-661-18.665, 18.671-18.675 and 18.691-18.692. For those freemasons that misuse the names and emblems, it is considered an un-masonic crime."[li]

"In 1994 the Grand Lodge of Idaho registered the square and compasses, restricting its use in that state. A special agreement with the Prince Hall Grand Lodge of Oregon, which warrants Prince Hall lodges in Idaho, permits them to use it also. The Grand Lodge of Scotland also has a copyright in place for the square and compasses incorporating the letter G. On August 3, 1994, the Masonic Foundation of Ontario officially registered the Grand Lodge logo, the square and compasses with the letter

---

[1] http://freemasonry.bcy.ca/grandlodge/trademark.html

[li] Grand Lodge of Michigan Constitutions and By-Laws Article XXXI, 4-

31 Sec. 2

G, with Consumer and Corporate Affairs, Canada, as published in Trade Marks Journal, Volume 41, and Number 2075. 7 This restricted the usage of the mark in Canada to regular Grand Lodges. More recently, in 2001, the Grand Lodge of New Zealand has also seen the need to register the masons' mark."[lii]

The best way to limit the activities of these spurious Masonic groups is the education of history to our members now, and especially those just entering our fraternity. There is not nearly enough education about the history of our Fraternity. Most Brethren either know some of the ritual that state we have existed since time immemorial, or from the days of Moses, or even from the time of Noah and the flood. This is fine for speculative history to add emphasis on our speculative heritage. But, we must ensure that we educate the organizational history of our Fraternity. Word of mouth is how the Fraternity has passed its most inner secrets of making good men better, it is also the way to educate on who is, or is not a Mason, and confidently educate those we met.

[lii] http://www.msana.com/focusarchives/focusapr01.asp

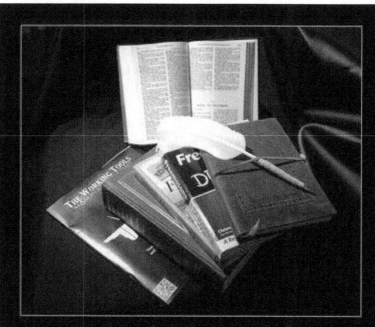

MASONIC EDUCATION

STUDY! Because just sitting through the minutes is not enough

Chapter 3

Regulating the Craft

Regularity in Freemasonry

A question must be asked as to how were Grand Lodges formed in so many parts of the world, and what composes a regular Grand Lodge in the first place? This is a question that is not asked by a Mason usually until after he has been made a Master Mason and he wishes to communicate with, or travel to other Lodges to visit and fellowship. If he has been made a Mason in a clandestine or irregular lodge, he will find that he cannot converse masonically, or visit many Masonic lodges here in the United States, or anywhere else in the world. The discovering of this can be discouraging to a newly raised Master Mason, excited at being told to take his place amongst the membership, entitled to all the rights and privileges as a Master Mason, which are to travel in to other Lodges and obtain knowledge he may not find in his own quarry, and then see the words become hollow.

The definition of what defines a lodge as being regular is left to each sovereign Grand Lodge to determine for its jurisdiction, under which it has subordinate lodges which hold allegiance to that Grand Lodge. Each Masonic Grand Lodge establishes its regulations in a Constitution and By-Law, which each Grand Lodge defines its own regulations. Most Grand Lodge's conform to the Ancient Usages, or old charges, in some capacity. These Ancient Usages have existed in the Fraternity, both unwritten and written, prior to its formal organizing in 1717 of the first Grand Lodge. One would find these lists of charges in Masonic manuscripts. These Old Charges (or Old Masonic Manuscripts) form the basis of modern Masonic Constitutions, and therefore, each Grand Lodge's jurisprudence contains elements of the charges.

For a Lodge to be considered regular in its forming and operation by what we will call "Mainstream Freemasonry," there are several indispensable items it must have in its possession, and certain practices that must be conformed too. A Lodge must have a certain number of Free and Accepted Masons assembled, the Volume of Sacred Law, i.e. a book of faith, and this is not restricted in most jurisdictions to a faith so if it represents a devotion to Deity. This book of Moral Law is to be on the lodge's altar so that Deity's presence is in the room, a chartered issued by a regularly formed Grand Lodge, and a constitution and by-law stating the laws of its governance.

These requirements to be met for a lodge to be recognized by Lodges of foreign jurisdictions, meaning lodges outside of the regulation of a subordinate Lodges Grand Lodge jurisdiction, evolved over time. From the *Regius Manuscript* in 1390, which mostly dictated the behavior of Free-Masons and their adherence to believe in God and worship in a church, and how one Mason was to regard another in treatment, to *Anderson's Constitutions* written in 1723. Instructions of the governing of the Craft evolved in an ever more specific way. To also be included in the noting of landmarks would be Albert Mackey and his compiled list of Masonic Landmark's, 25 of them to be exact, which denoted more specific rules for the government of a Lodge and the Craft, of which most lodges using a certain number of these, and some adopting them all.

In the world of Freemasonry, to be defined as regular, there are specific rules in determining the regularity of, or the forming of a Lodge. To learn what defines regularity and how to proceed with the formation of a Lodge, one needs to inquire with their jurisdictions Grand Lodge codes. The Most Worshipful Grand Lodge of the Ancient Free and Accepted Masons of the State of Illinois, just as every regular jurisdiction, has a very specific guideline to the forming of a Lodge for it to be regularly formed. In Illinois, a Lodge must have at least 20 regular Master Masons of a regular and recognized jurisdiction sign a petition to form a new lodge. The Master of the new Lodge must be deemed proficient by a Grand Lodge Lecturer to perform the opening and closing of a Lodge, proficiency in conferring the three Craft Lodge Degrees on a candidate in their entirety, and the reception of a Grand Lodge Officer. All of this must be done from memory as no ritual instruction book can be open in a constituted Lodge.

A Lodge also must have a safe, secure, and lawful place to meet, conforming to spaces needed to perform proper ritual; this also must be certified as suitable by a Grand Lecturer. It must confer the Degrees of Craft Freemasonry. Once the Lodge has operated under a dispensation from the Grand Master for a year, the Grand Master can elect to grant the lodge a Charter.

In North America, the regularity of a Grand Lodge is stated by a Commission on Information for Recognition, established in 1952. It gathers information on Grand Lodges seeking recognition and advises all the Grand Lodges that are members of the Conference of Grand Masters of Masons of North America. Its guidelines are as follows:

The standards of Recognition are:

"1.   Legitimacy of Origin
2.   Exclusive Territorial Jurisdiction, except by mutual consent and/or treaty.
3.   Adherence to the Ancient Landmarks ❖ specifically, a Belief in God, the Volume of Sacred Law as an indispensable part of the Furniture of the Lodge, and the prohibition of the discussion of politics and religion."[liii]

Number three in this list is universally followed by both all regular and most known clandestine Masonic jurisdictions alike. I speak from personal experience, having been a Past Master of what was known as St. Elmo's Lodge No. 70A, located in Kankakee, Illinois, a clandestine lodge, that the landmarks were followed closely. There was a requirement in a

[liii]http://recognitioncommission.org/2004/06/10/the-standards-ofrecognition/

belief in God, there was always a Holy Bible present at meetings, and they never discussed politics or religion in lodge. Also, there was always at least three Master Masons present, and there was a charter issued by a jurisdiction, empowering them to work. In my experience, many clandestine Lodges operated in the same manner, for the most part. So, why did I leave them and sought to become a regular mason? Number one and two of the standards of recognition would be that reason.

Legitimacy of Origin was not known to me as I petitioned to become a Mason in this clandestine Lodge. In fact, I had no idea there was such a thing. In 2004, I had no idea that Freemasonry was even talked about on the internet as I was not internet savvy yet. I had just bought my first computer. I came to befriend a man who was a Mason in the same manner many men, prior to Grand Lodges having websites had done. The gentleman carried himself in a very respectable way, he was married and had great kids, was a church going man and had a respectable profession. He never asked me to join, I inquired to him, stating my father was a Mason.

Time passed and after several attempts of asking to join, I was finally given a petition and then endured months of waiting for an interview. Patience was told to me to be my first lesson, which is the same lesson that should be told of all men when first petitioning a Lodge of Masons. After having passed through two interviews, one at home and the other blindfolded in front of a committee at the Lodge. I was then received into the Lodge and was initiated as an Entered Apprentice and passed to the degree of Fellow Craft the same night in November of 2004. Dinner followed at a nearby restaurant and all Brethren present congratulated me on entering the Craft.

As I think back to that night, it was a proud moment to me. I had set out to be what I had thought was the same path my father took in desiring to be a Mason, something I only knew of by seeing my father in my youth go off to meetings in his black suit. I was entering the same thing I had previously considered, but never felt I was mature enough to commit too. I was sitting at a table of Masons, of Brothers, who would teach me the secrets of Freemasonry. I was becoming a member of the Fraternity.

The next day I was given instruction by the Worshipful Master at the time, on the meanings of the symbolism of the many different emblems and working tools found within the two degrees. I was thoroughly impressed by what I was being taught. He did not teach me from a book. We spent countless hours talking about masonic symbolism and all that he had taught me came from his memory. The book, Crafts and its Symbols, by Allen Roberts, was given to me to study the first and second degree. This book, containing no ritual specifically, did explain much of the symbolism conveyed through Freemasonry, and matched what I had been taught thus far.

As I was not yet a Master Mason, I was not allowed to attend meetings, so the discussions with the Master was my only instruction. We would converse at both his house, and at the Lodge, about many masonic lessons through the study of Masonic symbolism. We did not cover history extensively though. I was told by some of that jurisdiction that we were Scottish Rite Masons and that the Prince Hall Affiliated Masons were York Rite. Prince Hall Masonry was not the path to go because they would have to come through us to become Scottish rite masons and obtain the 33rd Degree. This, of course, is not true. Prince Hall Masonry is a mirror image of the practice of mainstream Freemasonry as its origin is African Lodge no. 459, which received its charter from the Premier Grand Lodge of England. The Craft Lodge is composed of the three degrees of Freemasonry and the appendant bodies, the Scottish Rite and three bodies that encompasses the York Rite, and the Shrine, is available to Master Masons upon the acceptance of a petition for these bodies.

At his point, let us review some specifics about the practices of this lodge and jurisdiction in which I have begun my journey. It is deemed irregular in Masonic practice and origin to regular Masonic Jurisdictions. Specifically, they were not adherent to neither the ancient charges expressed in the previously mentioned Masonic manuscripts or the organizational practices of regular jurisdictions.

I was first placed into an ante-room. This room, located in the basement of the building, is basically a chamber of reflection, a practice used in the first degree of the Scottish rite Craft Degrees, the French Rite and some Traditional Observance Lodges. It is for the candidate to reflect upon his own mortality and come to terms with why he is seeking to become a member of the Fraternity. I am a huge supporter of the chamber of Reflection being used in ritual. Used in the proper way, it adds to the importance of the journey inward the candidate is preparing to take. By analyzing one's own desires to pursue Freemasonry and the teachings found therein, he focuses his mind and heart to enter the lodge and be exposed to information that can guide a man to the heights unimaginable in his own enlightenment.

However, this was not the experience I had. It was not quiet outside the door, as is required for a chamber of reflection. It was loud. Chairs were slammed on the floor. Firecrackers were placed against the outside wall and were exploding. Laughter filled the basement area as men participated in these antics. While I was writing my last will and testament, there was no silence, only distracting noises. In my heart, I do not believe that anyone was doing anything to harm me, only attempting to scare me to see if I had not come there truly seeking the secrets of Freemasonry.

While I was received on the point of a sharp instrument, I also received a wooden welcoming to my rear parts by several participants of the degree. During the ritual, part of the ceremony where one is shown to be duly and truly prepared to be made a Mason, meaning he is seen to be a man of proper age and as it is historically practiced where one cannot be made an operative mason without all his physical appendages, a man is seen to have the use of both arms and both legs. It must be noted that while some regular jurisdictions keep with this practice, most allow men who have lost the use of some limbs to still be made a Mason. Several men applied paddles to my backside, during both the first degree and second degree assuring I was prepared to be both an entered apprentice and a Fellow of the Craft.

Let us examine the problem with the application of physical hazing to the candidate during a Masonic Ritual during anytime, but specifically during the circumambulation. The word circumambulate itself means to circle by foot or walk around something. Masons walk the candidate around the Lodge for more than to visually ascertain if the candidate is physically prepared, it is also to allow the candidate and members present to consciously quiet their minds to prepare for this reverent embankment of enlightenment. All the positive energy of the room is drawn from the Brethren to the candidate. He is shut off from the profane world and is in meditation with words from the Volume of Sacred Law flows into his heart and the vision of who is to become is made central in his mind.

Hazing during the circumambulation in no way allows for a transition from the noise of the outside world to the serene pursuit of an opening of the subconscious. The first-degree ritual is designed to open the seat of consciousness thought, meaning the heart, to trust others in the pursuit of the acceptance of new experiences and information. This, in turn, removes the guards of inhibition from the thoughts of the mind and allows the mental transition from the focus of the nerves and butterflies of the unexpected, to the relaxed state of knowing one is in the company of trusted friends. This cannot happen while one's back side is being paddled.

Here is the history of this clandestine Lodge, noted on their website:

"St. Elmo Lodge was organized in 1947 in Kankakee, Il. working under St. John Grand Council A&ASRM which was also organized in 1947 working under The National Supreme Council A&ASRM. James Anderson was Worshipful Master at that time. The brothers didn't have a hall to meet so they meet at various location, after James Anderson, John Nallon was Worshipful Master, this was during the early 1950's, during this time a brother by the name of Joe Rivers Brown had joined the lodge, and it was during this time that a building would be donated to the lodge. It was moved to its present location 634 N.

Rosewood Ave, Bro. Herb Morris gave leadership to this move, Rev. James M. Smith, Pastor of Second Baptist Church helped dig the foundation and on May 27, 1956, he laid the corner stone. After Bro. Nallon and Bro. Brown had disagreement over some chairs, causing the lodge to split. Bro Nallon started another lodge in Riverwood which is known today as Sun River Terrace, he named it St. Elmo so there was two St. Elmo Lodges. Joe River Brown was named Worshipful Master and the lodge was named St. Elmo Lodge #70. Joe River Brown was the first black Kankakee County Sheriff Deputy and knew a lot of people, all the lodge's furniture was donated by the Kankakee Masonic Hall (Caucasian Masons), that knew Bro. Brown. During the late 1950's and early 1960's membership was up and down, and a new Prince Hall lodge was organized and some brothers left and joined. During the late 1960's and early 1970's the lodge was still having problems, it was during this time Bro. Sam Dunigan was Worshipful Master. In the late 70's and early 80's the lodge was closed, the Sister of Julia Chapter #70 OES was still meeting in the hall. It was early 1980 when Bro. T.J. Sanders 32° became Worshipful Master, and started to build up the membership. Under his leadership, the lodge started a scholarship fund giving away thousands of dollars to help students go to College. The lodge became famous for its fish fries and Bar-BQ dinners which supported those causes. Bro. Sanders holds the longest tenure as Worshipful Master of 18 years. In November 1998, he passed the gravel to Bro. Cameron Wells 32°. In 2002 Bro. Dezelle Crite32° became Worshipful Master serving until 2007; followed by Bro Charles Harper 32°, who was proceeded by Bro Darrick Brooks 32°, who was proceeded by Bro. Linell Jefferson 32°, up to now where the Ill Cameron Wells Sr. 33° is once again the current sitting Worshipful Master. For the past 65 years God, has truly blessed St. Elmo Lodge #916."[liv]

[liv] http://www.freewebs.com/stelmo70a/aboutus.htm

As you can read, my name is stated in this history. One might ask why my name would remain a part of this stated history. I originally did want my name removed as to remove me as a part of the Lodge's history. To deny that I was a member would be to deny both the good that was done, and the credibility of the experience I share now. One cannot change what was, they can only learn and progress.

Here is some photographic evidence of my former membership:

In this picture, taken in 2007 when I was the Senior Warden, notice the Scottish rite cap and robe, with the jewel of my office. This was taught to me to be the style of dress for an officer of a Scottish rite Craft Lodge. Those who were not officers wore red bordered aprons. While different regular jurisdictions offer a variety of dress as per their regulations, in Illinois, this is improper and thus another measure of being unregulated masonic practice.

There were the dues cards issued to me. Notice the different names of the masonic jurisdictions. From 2004-2007, it was the King Cyrus Supreme Council based in New York. From 2008 until I left, it was the American International Supreme Council. Both jurisdictions were named of the Scottish rite. This is a typical practice of some clandestine organizations as they attach themselves to credible masonic appendant bodies such as the Scottish rite.

Albert Pike wrote in his book, Morals and Dogma,

"Force, unregulated or ill-regulated, is not only wasted in the void, like that of gunpowder burned in the open air, and steam unconfined by science; but, striking in the dark, and its blows meeting only the air, they recoil and bruise itself. It is destruction and ruin. It is the volcano, the earthquake, the cyclone; --not growth and progress. It is Polyphemus blinded, striking at random, and falling headlong among the sharp rocks by the impetus of his own blows.

The blind Force of the people is a Force that must be economized, and managed, as the blind Force of steam, lifting the ponderous iron arms and turning the large wheels, is made to bore and rifle the cannon and to weave the most delicate lace. It must be regulated by Intellect. Intellect is to the people and the people's Force, what the slender needle of the compass is to the ship--its soul, always counselling the huge mass of wood and iron, and always pointing to the north."[lv]

[lv] Pike, A., 1871, Morals and Dogma, pg. 5, para. 1 and 2

This was a certificate I received in 2007 for my consistent contributions to the lodge in regards to effort to the Brethren, the Lodge, and the community. In the years leading to this certificate, I was involved in the scholarships for high school seniors, starting an Easter Egg Hunt for the community, and other assorted contributions.

MASTER MASON CERTIFICATE

ST. ELMO Lodge #70A

This certificate is awarded to:

Bro. Charles Harper

Who has proven himself as being proficient in the 1st, 2nd, and 3rd degrees of Freemasonry and has been initiated, passed and raised to the sublime degree of Master Mason and entitled to all the rights thereof. So Mote It Be

Issued by the American International Supreme Council
Ancient & Accepted Scottish Rite Masons

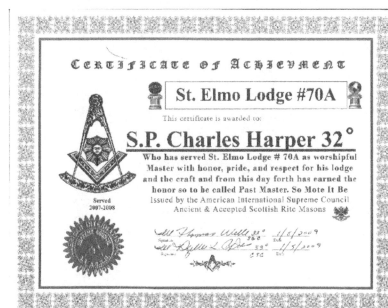

Certificate of Achievment

St. Elmo Lodge #70A

This certificate is awarded to:

S.P. Charles Harper 32°

Who has served St. Elmo Lodge # 70A as worshipful Master with honor, pride, and respect for his lodge and the craft and from this day forth has earned the honor so to be called Past Master. So Mote It Be

Served
2007-2008

Issued by the American International Supreme Council Ancient & Accepted Scottish Rite Masons

How appropriate are Albert Pike's words in regards to those who practice Freemasonry, unregulated, and promotes its interest, unaware that they themselves are not authorized masonically to do so and are not recognized by the world of Freemasonry as Masons? How do clandestine Masons answer? No one group owns Freemasonry and thus, we do not need permission from anyone to practice its rituals.

St. Elmo's Lodge no. 70A, 634 N. Rosewood, Kankakee, Illinois. Imagine paying $300.00 a year in dues, donating $500.00 during my time as a Fellow Craft to repair the roof. On years that the electricity was to be disconnected, I paid the $300.00 in dues at the beginning of the year and then assisted paying the dues of other Brethren who were not able. Not to mention other monies and time that was donated into the Lodge, and then realizing, you cannot speak to any other Masons or visit the Lodge not more than 5 minutes walking distance from yours.

No one needs permission from anyone if they wish to read the exposes of masonic ritual and practice imitating these rituals in their private dwellings. They do, however, need to be recognized as practicing regular Freemasonry per the ancient usages and practices of recognition if they wish to be received as Freemasons in the world. To charge men money to participate in what they believe they are a member of, and not informing them as to all the facts of their membership is fraud and is illegal in both New York State and Connecticut.

To charge men money to participate in what they believe they are a member of, and not informing them as to all the facts of their membership is fraud and is illegal in both New York State and Connecticut.

As I stood at the preparation door of my home Lodge, Kankakee Lodge No. 389, in April of 2010, already having told the members of what I went through in the clandestine Lodge during the ritual, I was told I could relax and clear my mind. The Mason at my side, while I was blind-folded, assured me I was in the hands of a trusted friend and that this was to be the beginning of a wonderful experience and that no physical harm was to happen or was even allowed in the ritual I was to undertake. A calming overtook me at that point. No one was yelling at me, questioning why I was there or who had possibly sent me to sneak into a Mason's Lodge, which had been the situation of the clandestine lodge. In the regular Lodge of Kankakee no. 389, I could calm my mind and it would be the most beautiful Masonic experience in my life, up and until that point.

Another part of the degree that is not a part of regular practices is that application of the cable-tow to the candidate in the first degree, when there are multiple candidates. Normally, there is a cable-tow applied to each candidate individually, whether there is one candidate or up to three candidates. The clandestine Lodge simply used one cable-tow and connected all the candidates together.

The use of the cable-tow by Masons is both a physical and symbolical use. Masonicworld.com gives a good symbolical description of the cable-tow stating, "The cable-tow, then, is the outward and visible symbol of a vow in which a man has pledged his life, or has pledged himself to save another life at the risk of his own. Its length and strength are measured by the ability of the man to fulfill his obligation and his sense of the moral sanctity of his obligation - a test, that is, both of his capacity and of his character."[lvi]   As the clandestine lodges symbolically attempts to attach each man to the other, both physically and symbolically, the practice is not regular in practice in most regular jurisdictions.

[lvi]http://www.chandlerlodge227.org/library/Cabletow.pdf

The physical use of the cable-tow is to lead a man out of the lodge, should he decide he does not want to submit himself to the obligation of a Freemason. Because he is blindfolded and has not been obligated as a Mason, he cannot see the inside of a tiled Lodge and the brethren therefore lead him out safely without him ever seeing a thing. Since I did not desire at this point to depart the Lodge, I was never lead out of the Lodge. I had up my mind that I wanted to be a Mason and I would do whatever was required of me to be made one. Was I afraid? Yes. But, I was determined to go through what my father had gone through so we could sit together, as Masons, in lodge, together.

Another part of the ritual, in both 1st and 2nd degrees I received in the clandestine Lodge that was irregular, was the amount of times I was circumambulated around the altar. There is a specific amount of times a candidate is taken around the altar per each degree. Without oversight and either a lack of understanding the purpose of this part of the ritual or a lack of control over the Lodge, this circling around the alter did not have a set number of times and allowed the participants on the outside of the circle, which in some instances was more than ten men, to paddle me and others many times. How this practice may have come about is up to speculation, being possibly passed from college fraternity hazing of the past and making its way into a Masonic lodge, to something that just "came about."

There are stories of actual hazing in Masonic Lodges in the past. Masons entering the lodge as an Entered Apprentice have had their chest pricked by a small sharp instrument in the same fashion as U.S. navy personal in the past having their naval qualification pins on their chest hit hard enough to leave permanent impressions on their chest. There was also the practice of a person being promoted from seaman to a 3rd class Petty Officer, they would receive punches all day from his shipmates in a congratulatory fashion. It did not feel congratulatory, but it was the custom or tradition long ago.

This practice of hazing, both in the U. S. Navy and in the Masonic Fraternity, were ceased for two reasons. One, people were getting injured and those that were not supportive of this hazing in fun filed lawsuits, leaving both the Navy and Masonic Fraternity liable for the injuries. Two, the image of hazing in the view of society is a negative one. Any organization seeking to promote a positive image should not have people being injured in the public news. How can you beat a man like a child and then call him your Brother and have the respect you?

Is this Lodge and its members, or the jurisdiction it belongs to, wrong for their practice of what they believe is freemasonry? The answer is actually-No. They are no more wrong in the desire to practice of Freemasonry than a jurisdiction that admits female members or one that removes the professed belief in Deity from their landmarks. So, one would ask what is wrong with the practices of this Lodge? Most of the men that belong, and possibly still belong to this lodge, were seeking to do good things for their community. The problem is that without belonging to a regular Grand Lodge, there can be no oversight to ensure regularities are followed. No regulation of activities performed in the name of Freemasonry. No consequences such as a removal of the charter which has consequences of the Masons no longer having membership and unable to masonically travel to other recognized lodges is not a possibility. The Lodge, if closed, can simply open another Lodge with the same members and incorporate it under a different name for tax purposes, or to sidestep court rulings. This Lodge may have had a grand lodge as their authority, but with no amity with any other Grand Lodge, there is nothing to enforce any adherence to regular masonic customs.

Amity

What is amity? Amity is when two Grand Lodges enter a contract of mutual recognition. Every Grand Lodge that wishes to allow its members to exercise their masonic rights of a master mason, to travel in foreign countries and work and receive a master's wage, enters a compact with another Grand Lodge that allows its members to speak masonically, and visit one another's Lodge. It is a way to enforce the adherence to the ancient craft usages.

As explained in the previous section of the understanding of regularity, all Grand Lodges formed in any territory must be organized with Lodges chartered by other Grand Lodges from other sovereign territories, formed in the same manner, where no lodges already exist. This repeated process of lodges being chartered by Grand Lodges, formed by Lodges of other jurisdictions, must originate from the mother Grand Lodge of the world, the Premier Grand Lodge of England, organized in 1717.

This is what the good men of St. Elmo Lodge no. 70A could never accept, unfortunately. This amity with other Grand Lodges, formed from the same origin, is what binds us together and ensures that all whom desire to visit and speak with other Masons, must have a compact of amity. It is somewhat of a security blanket of trust. If your Grand Lodge has been examined by the Grand Lodge of England to be sovereign on to itself, and the Grand Lodge it accepts as regular does the same process with another Grand Lodge, it creates a secure circle of trust in an international fashion that brings all Grand Lodges in the world into a world-wide circle of trust.

It reminds me of the movie, "Meet the Fockers." George Burns finds out that his daughter's boyfriend, Greg Focker, is informed that he was a former CIA agent. He is sitting on the bed when Greg wakes up, and he informs him that the secret of his background is out. He says to Greg, "You are now in what I like to call my circle of trust. You keep nothing from me, I keep nothing from you, and around and around we go. Once you break the circle you are out. And once you're out, you're out." This is the relationship that is kept with one Grand Lodge to another. If you keep to the ancient usages of the fraternity, following the useful forms and ceremonies, you can maintain your amity with all the Grand Lodges. If you violate these useful regulations, recognition can be withdrawn and you become isolated from the rest of the Masonic world.

A clandestine jurisdiction tends to have justifications for existing and can often seem to explain why they do not need to be recognized by the Masonic world. Although clandestine jurisdictions have the right to exist in most states as a business, they have no masonic authority to exist. I was taught in the clandestine lodge that recognition was not important and that one's obligation is what made him a Mason, not his recognition by another jurisdiction. This is both true and not true.

As Masons, we do learn that it is our obligation that makes us a Mason, or to be more specific, it is what makes us a member of the fraternity. It used to be in the Fraternity both overseas and in the United States that knowing one's obligation and the modes of recognition was all that was needed to prove oneself a Mason and enter a Lodge. It would not be until the Baltimore Convention of 1843, after the anti-masonic period, that security of the Lodges from cowans and eavesdroppers would be tightened as the secrets of our passes, tokens and handshakes had been exposed for some time.

In 1843, the Committee on General Regulations would put forward measures that the attending Grand Lodges would adopt to ensure continuity and continuation of the Craft. One of these measures proposed and adopted the following year would be to protect the fraternity from unworthy men claiming to be Masons. It recommended that "certificates of good standing" of visiting brethren be made available by their Grand Lodges.[lvii]

This would shield the Institution and furnish the widow and orphan of a deceased brother the best evidence of their claim upon the Fraternity. (1st Dues Cards) Measures were being taken to maintain and protect the integrity of the membership of regular masonic jurisdictions.

I was raised in the clandestine Lodge, St. Elmo Lodge no. 70A, on June 4, 2005 in Kankakee, Illinois. I did not receive a dues card. I did not receive an apron. It was never explained to me that I would not be able to visit other Lodges for masonic fellowship. I did not sign the constitution and by-laws of the Lodge. I received a bloody forehead, a sore rear end and a small book to register the payment of my monthly dues of $25.00 a month. The only thing my book could be used for is to show I gave money to the Lodge to sit in the meetings. I could not gain entry to any regular Lodge, which included four in a five-mile radius from where the clandestine lodge stood.

Access to just and regular masonic lodges was denied.

As Masons, we know that we recognize each other by certain signs we use, secret grips, passwords and such. As in the days of the stone guilds and the traveling of the operative stone masons of the craft in search of work, arrival at a work site and the granting of work would depend on the proving of possession of having mastered one's craft. To be recognized as a master of his craft, a mason would prove his credentials by certain a certain grip, given to the overseer of the craft. He would from that day forward be recognized as a master of HIS craft.

As the historical documents, we have come to find, manuscripts illustrating the ancient charges of the craft, showing the transition of the operative guilds or lodges into speculative, the standard of recognizing another traveling man had not changed much. Speculative Masons in the mid-1600's still used a grip to recognize another as a speculative mason, but due to the desire to protect the freedom to exchange ideas in a safe environment, free from cowans or eavesdroppers, which are those that are just curious or antagonist of elevating one's mental process, more depth was added to proving one was a mason, and thus gaining the recognition by others as a Free-Mason. When we state recognition today of another man or Masonic Jurisdiction, we are specifically referring to the recognizing a man or Masonic jurisdiction as a conforming to the standards of recognition, established by each sovereign Grand Lodge in its territory, usually consisting of Legitimacy of Origin, Territorial Sovereignty and Conformity to the Ancient Landmarks.

As the attraction of Freemasonry grew, and with more and more lodges being created without oversight throughout Ireland, Scotland and England, and other countries, declaring themselves speculative Masonic lodges, amongst other necessities needed to practice and revive masonry after Sir Christopher Wren's departure of attention from the Craft in the south of England in 1716, a need grew to establish a network in which each lodge would recognize another as keeping with the same practices and standards. The four lodges that met in London at the Goose and Gridiron, the Crown, the Apple Tree Tavern and the Rummer and Grapes Tavern, met at the Apple Tree Tavern in February of 1717, voted the oldest Mason present as Grand Master and formed the first Speculative Masonic Grand Lodge.

It would only be 34 years later that another dominant Grand Lodge would form in England, dissatisfied with practice of Freemasonry of the affectionately known "Knife and Fork" masons of the premier Grand Lodge. Though it has been speculated that this was a schism, author John Belton, in his book, *The English Masonic Union of 1813: A Tale of Antient and Moderns*, as he relates to words of John Heron Lepper of why Scotch Masons stating why they left their home land stating, "Perhaps we should countenance the thought that immigrant Irish and Scots Masons were not finding themselves welcomed into Lodges of Englishmen and that they did what all immigrant communities do- they simply formed their own societies to meet their needs."[lviii] None of the Lodges that formed the Ancients Grand Lodge of England in 1751 held allegiance to the Premier Grand Lodge.

Now, here is the dilemma. At the same time the two Grand Lodges are operating in London, England, until the merger of 1813, the Grand Lodge of Scotland and Ireland are growing in membership. So, which Grand Lodge in England do they "recognize" as Freemasons? Adding to the dilemma of who to recognize as Masons in England, the two Grand Lodges in Ireland, Dublin and Ulster, battling it out in Ireland at the same time for territory! The only solution to the problems of who to recognize as Masons in both countries were for the Masons to unite. One had to subdue their ego and pride and allow the best interest for the promulgation of the craft to prevail. The problems that were caused by the forming of two grand lodges of masons in the country of Ireland separated, instead of uniting men. As John Belton states, "The victory at Waterloo and the

[lviii] Belton, J. 2011, The English Masonic Union of 1813: A Tale of Antient and Moderns, Arima Publishing

defeat of Napoleon were in the future, the country was fractious and the example of Masonic insurrection in Ireland was a warning to England."[lix]

This problem in Great Britain of the separation of the Craft before 1814 is a clear indication of how important it was for a Masonic Grand Lodge to be recognized as the authority in its territory. Authority in a territory is paramount to the Fraternity of Freemasons as it establishes uniformity of all Masonic practices as in conforming to the ancient charges written beginning with the Regius Manuscript of 1390 and continuing forward to today in each Grand Lodges written constitution. Each Grand Lodge in its territory, in the United States this is designated by the states boundary lines, must have governance or authority if you will, over all the Masons of that territory and be "Recognized" as such.

This leads us to the benefits of recognition. In 1723, James Anderson was ordered to write what would be the first constitution and by-laws of the Fraternity. It was also during this time that Grand Master ordered that all Lodges under the jurisdiction of the Grand Lodge of England be authorized to initiate Masons, but only at Grand Lodge, to ensure uniformity in the ritual, could a Lodge raise a man to be a Master Mason. All Lodges under the authority of the Grand Lodge of England, and later the United Grand Lodge of England after the merger, the Grand Lodge of Scotland and Ireland, all ensured the work was done in the same manner and recognized each other as doing such. Because they all recognized the way they all conducted ritual work in making masons, men could travel and visit lodges in the others jurisdiction, as operative stone masons had, to witness and learn from the others similar, but varying ritual work.

[lix] http://www.freemasonry-freemasonry.com/arnaldoGeng.html

As Master Masons, a question often asked of us is why we were so induced to become Master Masons. We entered the Craft so that we could travel in foreign countries, as our operative ancestors had, and work in the quarries to earn a Master's wage. Our passes and grips prove our status as a Master of the Craft, showing we had apprenticed under another such Master of the Craft. Today, our labors are not done in the quarries, filled with rough stone, shaped with our tools by our hands, but in the visitation of a Lodge outside of our own, to work our minds as spiritual stones, shaping and perfecting them with the tools of challenged thought amongst trusted Brethren.

The plethora of friendships that have been made, the history and esoteric books that have been composed about Freemasonry, is a by-product of Masons being able to visit foreign jurisdictions, recognizing the other as keeping to the same standards and practices of Ancient Craft Freemasonry. Without recognition, a Mason is isolated from his Brethren. He is limited, confined and restricted to his own area. He cannot share speculated ideas with different Brethren outside of his confined area, enabling him to hear new input, expand and improve his complete understanding of concepts or to see if his ideas are within due bounds of other great minds existing within the Masonic community. Like a person fishing in the same old pond, if he ever expects to experience any assortment in his fish diet, he must expand his search and experience fishing in some different ponds.

Get the picture?

Clandestine Mason from a clandestine Grand Lodge

Regular Mason from a regular and recognized Masonic jurisdiction

Recognition serves to exclude those whose practices may not be of the same Masonic origin or meet the same standards of ancient practices. It serves as a deterrent to un-masonic or irregular practices. The Grand Orient of France, "At its general assembly held on September 13, 1877, it proclaimed that it was unnecessary for a Candidate for Freemasonry within its jurisdiction to declare any belief in the Great Architect of the Universe or in a True and Living God."[lx] All regular, and recognized to be Masonic Grand Lodges, requires a belief in a Supreme Being, not allowing any atheist to be made a Mason. This is of course not to establish the Fraternity as some sort of religion, but an obligation to the highest moral and ethical standards is taken on a book of one's faith, and as such, binds a man to his obligation. A jurisdiction not adhering to this ancient charge cannot be recognized as practicing Freemasonry to the standards established more than three centuries ago. The Grand

[lx] http://www.freemasonry-freemasonry.com/arnaldoGeng.htm

Orient of France has not been recognized as practicing regular Freemasonry since 1877, and still does not to this day.

Less known Masonic Jurisdictions throughout the United States and England operate as clandestine jurisdictions and are not recognized. Among these are Co-masonry known as Le Droit Humain, which allow both men and woman to be masons and exist in many countries, though the numbers of their membership are not known. While these Grand Lodges exist, they do make clear that they are not an all-male organization. They state they operate in the same manner as regular U.S. Grand Lodges, but they cannot be recognized as regular Lodges because the fraternity since its creation has been traditionally all male.

There are many clandestine African-American Grand Lodges, existing predominantly in the major metropolises of almost every state in the United States. Per the Phylaxis Society, there are more than 57 clandestine Grand Lodges operating in Chicago, Illinois alone. This number is similar in many major cities of the United States. These Grand Lodges remain clandestine not only because they do not seek recognition of regular Grand Lodges, they would not qualify for recognition anyway. They do not have authentic Masonic origins in their forming, as the subordinate lodges that they are comprised of were formed by incorporation and not chartered by an existing regular Grand Lodge from an already established different territory.

These clandestine Grand Lodges often fool men into believing they are authentic as they attach the acronyms of A.F.& A.M. and other forms, attempting to attach themselves to the Free and Accepted or Ancient Free and Accepted Masons of pre-1813 England., to their names and displaying the emblem most recognized as Masonic, the square and compass, to their identities. But, these clandestine Grand Lodges, who take advantage of men unknowing of what comprises a Grand Lodge as regular, often abuse the trust instilled in them by charging absorbents amount of money for various degrees as degree peddlers have done during the days predating the first Grand Lodge and soon after the organizing of the mother Ancient and Accepted Scottish Rite Supreme Council of the world in 1801, Charleston, South Carolina. There are stories of hazing and the promise men, after the payment of all the degrees, can obtain entrance into any Lodge in the world. Men have found out after knocking on the door of a regular Lodge that they have been taken advantage of and are not recognized as Masons at all.

Since recognition was first established by the Grand Lodge of Massachusetts to the Most Worshipful Prince Hall Grand Lodge of Massachusetts in 1995, all but nine Grand Lodges in the United States have extended recognition. The lack of a recognition agreement in these nine remaining states between the Grand Lodge and Prince Hall Grand Lodge leads to speculation by some in public debate forums, that it assists in the rise of clandestine Grand Lodges forming in the African-American community because if not all Prince Hall Grand Lodges are recognized as Masons by the existing Grand Lodges in their state, then recognition must not truly be needed to operate in another Grand Lodges territory. The lack of recognition brings me to the bigger problem of the regular Masonic bodies withdrawing recognition from one another.

The Masonic Fraternity is known as the universality of man under the fatherhood of God. It is a world-wide fraternity. A man made a Mason in a regularly constituted Lodge in California can go as far east as Japan, as far south as Australia and as far north as Alaska, and visit and sit in a tyled Masonic Lodge and be greeted with fraternal friendship, brotherly love and civil hospitality. As in every lodge, Masons meet on the level because no matter the titles, wealth, nationality, creed or race, we are all the same and all have been made Master Masons the same manner. By the very virtue of the establishment of recognition as our security from being involved with men who are not upright masons, we are confident when we visit a lodge; we are amongst Brothers, friends and family, a place of trust where there are no strangers, just brothers we haven't met yet.

When we do not extend recognition to Masonic bodies or we withdrawal it from them, we are stating to the world that these men have been investigated and found out not to be Masons, nor do we desire them to be seen by the world as upright men, Freemasons. When recognition does not exist, it is stating that the practices of these individuals of whatever jurisdiction they may belong to are not in the best interest of the fraternity to associate within fraternal relationships.

When there is no recognition of a jurisdiction, we are saying to the world that these men are not Freemasons, period. Recognition is a safeguard from those that do not adhere to Masonic Standards existing from the organizational inception of the world's first Masonic Grand Lodge. It is not to be extended lightly, or withdrawn lightly. It shows the world Masonic unity, or separations, that exist in the same capacity of any other organization.

The Masonic Fraternity is not like any other organization. It has benefits to being a member. Its purpose is to take good men and make them better. It allows the ability of a man to learn through ritualistic means, symbolism that can take him to the truths he seeks in a trusted environment where this search can be had without judgment. It does not exist to separate men. It exists to unite men under a common belief that through a sacred trust, ideas of humanity, ethics and moral philosophy can be expounded upon and shared to make men realize their own inner potential of existence. It exists to bring men together who can best work and best agree.

As has been shown since the early formation of our fraternity, coming together for the best of the fraternity has always resulted in positive relationships across the globe. A difference of opinion has, and always will, existed amongst good men. It is the overcoming of these differences that make men better, within the scope of the moral law existing in the foundation the fraternity was established upon. Recognizing another man as a mason is a great feeling shared by many Masons every day. The common bond we share can barely be expressed in mere words.

Use the extending and withdrawing of recognition wisely for the world is always watching to see how Freemasons handle themselves, as our actions have always been markers of the world's progress. How we act together within the confines of our Lodges will be displayed in the public to see by the behavior we exhibit. So, what do we do? Do we let society radiate into our lodges and become the trestle-boards we learn by, or do we show restraint, a subduing of passion and a swallowing of pride for the sake of the whole? How will we show the world that merit is the title of our privileges and why we, as Freemasons, exist to help humanity by the exemplary character we exhibit? We meet on the Level leaving pride outside of our doors. We Act upon the Plumb and subdue our passions. We part upon the square Brethren, leaving our Brother in the best condition to succeed. Sometimes, the simplest answer lies before us.

The Fraternity of Freemasons, the original level playing field.

Charles M. Harper Sr.
www.freemasonryinblackandwhite.com

Travel in Foreign Countries

I wonder how many Brothers realize the impact of that right for a Master Mason, in having the ability to visit a Master Mason's Lodge in a foreign jurisdiction, or what that statement truly denotes. "To work in foreign countries and earn a Master's wage."

In the days of the operative Mason, before speculative Freemasonry was organized in 1717, it is taught to us that an operative mason was taught the trade of a stone mason by becoming an apprentice to a journeyman. After his apprenticeship was over and he had mastered his trade, he was given the password and grip to prove he was a journeyman to other stonemasons. He was therefore free to travel to foreign countries and earn a wage. The grip and password weeded out those who had not mastered his craft from gaining employment under false pretense. Thus, the integrity of the trade was protected.

"The Freemasons worked according to a set of rules and regulations of their own, centuries old, among them being Landmarks, and such questions of organization or of work arose in any given Lodge were settled according to those rules; and since the same rules were in force wherever Freemasons worked, and each Apprentice and Fellow was under an oath never to violate them, it was this body of rules which gave its unity and consistency to a Fraternity which had no national organization or national officers. And until the fourteenth century, they did not even have permanent local organizations, and which at the same time preserved its rules and trade secrets in the memory of its members and taught them to Apprentices by word of mouth."[lxi]

Because the stonemason could travel away from his homeland in his protected trade, it enabled him to learn differences in how he labored compared to other workman in other lodges in other countries. Although basic knowledge was similar, the application of formation of cathedrals had small differences from one area to another depending on the architect and his training. The structure was engineered with the basic principles of weight distribution with right angles, horizontals, and perpendiculars. But, the sculpture and layout varied per the vision laid out on the trestle board for each building by the designer.

A humble master, who always sought to better his skill, enjoyed traveling. It allowed him to expand his skills by obtaining knowledge of techniques that were different than the ones he had already mastered. So, by traveling, versus staying in one area his whole career, he could better appreciate the potential of the creativity that dwelled inside him. He could better express his ability and individuality by the reflection of his collective intake of the many ways of creating a masterpiece he witnessed in so many other different places.

We, as speculative masons, are afforded the same ability and privilege. Through our system of defining regularity and

[lxi] http://www.themasonictrowel.com/Articles/History/other_files/ope

rative_freemasonry.htm

establishing recognition with foreign jurisdictions, we are taught how to prove ourselves as masters of our speculative trade. The continued use of passwords, grips and add to that signs and dues cards, allows us the opportunity to visit other Lodges throughout the world and experience the differences in ritual and the varied personalities of different Lodges.

This experience of visitation benefits us in many great ways using reflection. The journey of betterment of a man in the application of the lessons we learn in Freemasonry is only possible when he reflects on his past experiences in life with trusted others and compares them with the ideals of what he envisions himself to become. But, if he only exposes himself to only his Lodge and the members contained therein, the reflection of his behavior is biased. There will come a point when one will realize that if he remains in his lodge, secluded from the rest of the masonic world, there is no outside input to test if any changes in his thoughts or actions in being a mason, are within due bounds of ALL mankind.

Although we are not stonemasons, roughing designs out of stone with the physical tools of this tradesman, we continue to shape our spiritual self with the symbolism of the tools this workman used. Each Lodge uses the application of symbolism in ever slightly different ways. It may be the way that a lecturer might deliver a charge, or the passion a Worshipful Master who gives an obligation that might charge you to make a change in yourself that had not occurred to you before.

You may share some insight of what a certain meaning in Freemasonry may mean to you. A more experienced Mason may happen to point out something that hadn't occurred to you. Or, you may teach an older Mason something he had not thought of before by the benefit of fresh perspective.

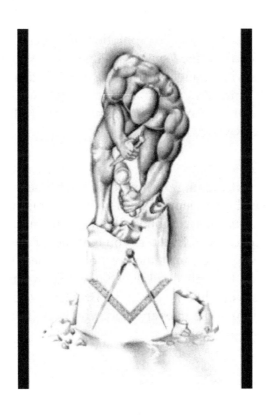

These many examples of the ability to share thoughts and experiences for becoming a better man are made possible by Lodge visitation. We must not allow ourselves to become comfortable in staying within the confines of just our Lodge. It truly limits our exposure to great learning and expanded fraternal friendships. To travel in foreign countries IS to visit other Lodges than your own. To earn a master's wage IS to gain knowledge and experience due to visiting these other Lodges, and reflecting on the shared information in your visit. This enables you to gain a more well-rounded insight into your own thoughts and actions. Which, the result of an improved self is benefited not by just yourself, but your relationship with your family, friends and even your co-workers.

Remember, the very nature of a Lodge is for like-minded men to come together for the promotion of shared thoughts and ideas in a trusted confined space. To know that you can share your opinions with strangers, of whom aren't because we are all bound by the same obligation of assistance to a worthy Brother Mason, is one of THE most valuable privileges a Master Mason can take full advantage.

So, the next time you are out of town on a business trip and find yourself flipping the remote in your hotel room, find the local Lodge and give them a call to visit. One might find, as I often do, that the fraternal bond of being a Freemason allows an instant connection with Brothers you have never met before. It seems that every time I visit another Lodge, I meet Brothers for the first time and it feels like I have known them forever. And before long, anyone like I, will find a Brother, a friend, and a home away from home in every place you visit. For no good man is ever traveling alone.

Chapter 4

Social Issues

Racism in Freemasonry

There was extensive slavery in the coastal districts of North Africa, fed by white captives sent there by Algerian corsairs. In many countries of the Old World and the New, the slavery of the Negro was a common fact. In America, that style slavery was yet to grow into a great and terrible vested interest. In the first half of the eighteenth century British children-white children- could be legally sold into slavery in America. But, the world was ceasing to be quite complacent in the matter, and, particularly in England, there arose a clear call that the whole dreadful business should be brought to an early end. This, alas, did not prevent Englishmen from taking a leading part in the shipment of African Negroes across the Atlantic.

No slave could exist in England after 1772, although, as already said, complete emancipation by Act of Parliament did not come until 1833. Near the end of the eighteenth century any slave reaching the soil of Scotland was a freeman.

Question: If Freemasonry came from Great Britain, and slavery did not exist after 1772, meaning Black men like John Pine could, and were made Masons, why do some hold the belief that one should not seek Freemasonry from the white man when Black men were easily made masons in England, Scotland or Ireland right before Prince Hall was made a Mason in an Irish Chartered Lodge in 1775? Does it not make sense that it was only American Freemasons that denied Black men to be made Masons? The passage indicates that even before the uniting of the two prominent Grand Lodges in England, black men were just as welcome as any other race to be made masons in a Lodge in Great Britain.

If we were to place ourselves in the late 1700-early - 1800's in the United States, being black men looking at other black men become Masons and spread this masonry, why not do it in the same fashion as Prince Hall? More than likely, this opportunity did not exist after the declaration of America's independence from England. So, due to slavery still in full swing in the United States, especially before the Civil War, the only way a free Black man could become a Mason was to seek out Prince Hall and one of his Lodges and be made a Mason; or establish their own. Who existed to tell them otherwise? An overwhelming majority of whites would not speak to blacks as equals; much less explain things about Freemasonry to them. Also, White grand lodges did not, and would not, recognized Prince Hall as a mason, nor his lodges, regardless of his charter from the Grand Lodge of England, which granted him the same rights and privileges as the white masons. If the white masons did not see Prince Hall as a regular Free and Accepted Mason, his status as a Mason in another black man's mind, was worth nothing.

The clandestine Grand Lodges that have existed from the late 1800's, more than likely, started in this fashion. The thought of, "If they don't accept you as Masons anyway, what is in the validity of a charter from England, the same as the white lodges possess, if they do not accept you as a Mason?" They have a point. If one's charter to practice Masonry, derived directly from the same place as everyone else's charter has been derived, doesn't grant one recognition as a regular mason, then why go to Prince Hall or one of the Lodges his Lodge chartered, for the rights to practice masonry?

Everyone that practices the same Masonry, meaning knowing the ritual, grips and passwords, should be able to start their own lodge, right? If the future of Freemasonry was to always be segregated, one may have a legitimate reason to establish a Grand Lodge where they deem. However, the practice of Freemasonry, in and of itself, is not to practice segregation, even if some Grand Lodges are perceived too.

It could be concluded that Prince Hall saw this future back in 1784. He sought the same rights and privileges as the white masons in America because he believed that all were equal, even if racism blinded most Americans in that time. He did not cheat the system, having to possibly justify his actions later with the same fallacy in logic that criminals use to justify their actions when breaking the laws of civil society. He followed the Masonic Law practiced by the mainstream Masonic World. To allow clandestine Grand Lodges, specifically in the African-American communities in America, to continue to exist, is to undermine the future of race relations in a Fraternity where the color of one's skin, the professed religion and the status of a man's profession, has no meaning within tyled doors.

Clandestine Masonry, because it is unregulated, serves to feed into the minds of men with Neanderthal type mentalities towards men of different races, as a point of reference of what may be if "We" let "Them" in. It feeds into bigoted mindsets because more pictures of men, claiming to be masons, holding up signs in the same fashion gangs hold up their signs in a supposed lodge, displaying derogatory behavior that would never be authorized in a regular lodge, etc., are abundant on the internet. Clandestine Masonry is regarded as such because there has been no investigation done, via a request for recognition from a regular and recognized Grand Lodge by an unrecognized Grand Lodge, to determine its practices.

In the 21st century, many African-American clandestine Masons insist that they have established their lodges and Grand Lodges in the same Prince Hall did, but this is simply not true. These clandestine lodges and grand lodges were formed by men who may or may not even have been masons, may or may not have been made a mason in a regular lodge, and sought to establish their own lodges, for monetary gain or because they were discontent with the practices of the lodges where they were previously a member.

On April 28, 2010, I became the first African-American raised to the Sublime Degree of Master Mason in my Masonic Lodge, Kankakee Lodge No. 389 under the jurisdiction of the Most Worshipful Grand Lodge of Ancient Free and Accepted Masons of the State of Illinois. I was not the first to petition, just the first to petition and be accepted. Are you just as curious as to why as I was after I had found this out? Well, I asked the Past Masters. I asked, "Why aren't more men of different ethnicities petitioning this Lodge?" The Past Master told me that he didn't know. He knew of one gentleman before that had petitioned, but he was not accepted. As regular Masons know, the ballot of a Mason is secret and cannot be investigated as to how one votes. So, we sat and speculated on it together, both gathering memories of hearsay and speculation as to why this has not happened many times before.

To give insight why I would be the first man of African-American descent to be made a regular Master Mason in my Lodge, it is important restate that I was previously made an irregular Mason in a lodge regarded as clandestine by the Grand Lodge of Illinois, the Most Worshipful Prince Hall Grand Lodge of Illinois and every other regular and recognized Masonic Grand Lodge in the world. This lodge was unlike the ones many may have heard about in major cities of the United States that simply beat their candidates take large sums of money and give them nothing in return. No, this Lodge was different.

The Worshipful Master at the time, in 2004, was incredibly knowledgeable about many aspects of Freemasonry as far as symbolism. In fact to this day, the major thing that I feel he was not well informed about is what makes a Lodge regular and the accurate information of the progression of Freemasonry as we most accurately verify with the *Regis Manuscript,* and the manuscripts subsequently presented since then, the descriptive accounts of men being made speculative Masons in Operative Lodges, specifically in Scotland at the Lodge of Edinburgh No.

1, in Edinburgh, Scotland, and the importance of Masonic Recognition with foreign jurisdictions. So, what is it about my masonic beginnings that may tend to explain the possible misinterpretations between racist comments one may hear in society and the cultural differences that may be perceived as racist in this racially delicate spoken society of America?

In 2004, I was initiated, passed and raised in a year, having to show proficient knowledge in the study of masonic symbolism in Freemasonry that was unlike that of catechisms to prove proficiency in regular Lodges. As both an Entered Apprentice and a Fellow Craft, I had to memorize the symbolism attached to almost every masonic symbol one would find in a Masonic Lecture of a regular Lodge. It was not that I had to know every symbol, but I never knew which symbolism I was to be questioned on. I did not necessarily study masonic history of the organization of the Fraternity of Freemasons though. I do not feel it was excluded purposely. Perhaps, it was not taught to be important to those who were instructing me, and like it goes in even regular lodges, if one does not teach certain information to the student, and explain the importance, it goes untaught and unquestioned. We knew Freemasonry came from England, but its legitimate travel to the United States was never really discussed… until later in my journey.

So, why did I petition this lodge instead of the regular Lodge located in the same city? Frankly, I did not even know the regular Lodge even existed. Like many men who desire to become Masons, I saw a man wearing a jacket with the Masonic emblem of the square and compass on it and sought out to become a member. I was not aware of regularity or recognition and quite honestly, I thought Freemasons were a secret society and it did not even occur to me to search on the internet for more information. But more importantly, I petitioned this lodge because their members were African-American.

I am bi-racial, White and African-American, but this was the culture I knew and was comfortable around. It had nothing to do with race itself, with my mother being white and my father being African-American. It had more to do with identity. I identified with African-American exclusively then and so ensued my pursuit with the trust of my culture.

I knew so little of the Fraternity that I did not question why the Lodge only had African-Americans as members. I had met many Prince Hall Masons in the past and truly did not even know what Prince Hall Masonry was or that it was a Masonic jurisdiction all its own. I had only previously met African-American Masons. As I found out years later after doing considerable research into Freemasonry, the Fraternity is composed of every ethnicity on the planet and had Lodges in every free society on the planet Earth. So, my journey begs the question, was it out of a prejudicial nature that I did not seek out a lodge of predominately white membership, was it out of ignorance, or was it out of a comfort level that was relative to cultural differences?

Initially, I sought membership in this Lodge because it was the only visible Lodge I had seen where I lived. It being all African-American added to the security that everything was on the level because that was my own culture. Also, they were Freemasons, and from what I heard, all Freemasons are men one can trust.

It was not until my third year as a clandestine Mason, 2006 that I started to have questions about my membership being accepted by all Masons. Upon rekindling a relationship with my father by showing him I was a Mason, and he asking what Lodge I was made a Mason in, did I ever doubt my Masonic affiliation. My Dad, who never lies, completely rocked my Masonic world. He told me to read books on masonic history and organizational structure. I became obsessive with the history of Freemasonry. I compared notes from every book I read to any other book, leaving nothing open to interpretation. By 2008, a year had gone by and I had called the Medinah Shriners, several Valleys of the Scottish rites and several Grand Lodges to inquire about my affiliation, and with the more than 20 books I had read, I concluded that I was sure that I was not a Mason in the eyes of mainstream Masonry.

With my Masonic world rocked, I know had to begin the task of finding a regular Lodge to petition. My father's Lodge was more than a 40-minute drive from my house. I wanted to be active so, that would not work. The Prince Hall Lodge in my city met 40 minutes outside of my city, which would not work as well. I asked around about the Lodge in downtown Kankakee, Illinois, which I had noticed once I began to look for a regular Lodge to petition, but most people I asked, African-American's and clandestine Masons as well, said that they heard it was a racist Lodge because they have never had a Black person as a member. One person I asked even remarked that he believed they did not even met there anymore.

Almost a year would go by and it was by chance a friend of mine, a Hispanic friend who was also in the same situation I found myself in, saw gentleman coming out of the Lodge and he stopped them and asked them for a petition. He told them about me and they told him to send me up there. I called the Grand Lodge and gave them my information. Within a week, the Master of the Lodge called me and invited me to dinner.

After a couple months of dinners and discussion, my petition was filled out, signed by me and vouched for by other members of the lodge, and submitted. The investigation at my home followed. I was balloted on and was received. By April 28, 2010, after posting proficiencies in the preceding degrees, I was made a regular Master Mason and could take full benefits of the rights and privileges of one and travel to as many Lodges as my time would permit.

Now, I digress to the conversation with the Past Master about why no African-American had ever been a member before. This Past Master and many of the members of the Lodge were personal friends with the Past Masters and other members of the Prince Hall Affiliated Lodge that met in Kankakee, True Lodge No. 136, prior to them moving the place of their stated meeting out of town, which they had been for doing several years. No one outside of the regular Masonic membership of the area would know of this because the Brethren of my Lodge and that of the Prince Hall Lodge do not communicate masonically with the members of my previous clandestine Lodge. For me, that would explain why the clandestine Masons would have derived that my Lodge members might be racist. They never saw any African-American men come in or out of the temple, they did not know when the lodge even met and never conversed with any of the Masons.

To further perpetuate the false assumption that the members of my lodge were racist, the clandestine Lodge had a Masonic Ball while I was still a member. They invited every Masonic Lodge they could find in the phone book. No Lodge replied to the offer for attendance. At the event, which took place in early 2009 while I was a member and where I delivered the opening speech to the event, some Masons did show up that had heard about it, but they were unaware that the Lodge placing the event was clandestine. The event was public so actually, the Brothers did no wrong by being present, they showed up because they saw that it was masonic and came to support Masonry. One of the white Brothers even remarked to the local paper that he did not care if the Masons were green, purple, blue, black, or orange, he was there to support. He did not know they were clandestine.

St. Elmo Lodge 70a 2009

The following Monday after the event, an article about the festivities was published in the city paper. Members of the clandestine Lodge made public comments in the City newspaper, an article called, "Putting Racial Differences Aside," by Antonio Young of the Kankakee Daily Journal of the March 7, 2009 event, quoted remarks by a member of the Clandestine Lodge, saying that he was "thrilled about the nearly 500 people that showed up at the event, but he was disappointed that only three of the many invited white Masons from the area showed up."[lxii]

I was had a conversation with some of the members of the Lodge about the article and the possible negative ramifications of the message that was conveyed if we were to truly close the gap of the racial divide. Personally, I was disgusted by the fashion in which members confronted the mainstream Masons publically, whether one felt they did not attend for racial reasons or not. If the lack of attendance was racially motivated, would making such remarks encourage the other Masons to open a line of communication? If we were wrong as to why they could not attend, we would look like fools. There would be no possibility of meeting on any level to discuss any working together in the community, I thought and said. Of course, if one considers cultural relativity, it is understandable the confidence in this ideology being presented relative to the history of race relations in the past and present. However, A Mason should find this ideology sickening, which he should then positively and friendly, confront any brother he sees displaying it.

[lxii] Young, A. 2009. Putting Racial Differences Aside, Kankakee Daily Journal

JOURNAL Serving Kankakee, Will, Iroquois, Ford, Grundy & Livingston counties.

Putting racial differences aside

03/24/2009, 2:18 pm
Comment on this story

By Antonio Young
ayoung@daily-journal.com
815-937-3385

The mood was festive when St. Elmo Lodge 70A held its first "Brothers and Sisters United" Masonic ball nearly two weeks ago at the Quality Inn & Suites in Bradley.

The March 7 gala was held to encourage men and women from area Masonic and Order of the Eastern Star lodges to fellowship, regardless of their affiliation or letters.

Robert Chapman, treasurer for St. Elmo -- a predominately black lodge based in Kankakee -- was thrilled that about 500 people attended the event. But there was one disappointment: Only three of the many invited white Masons from the area showed up.

Beginning in January, Chapman mailed invitations to predominately white lodges in Kankakee, Chebanse, St. Anne, Peotone. The men of St. Elmo hope to unite with those lodges to do future community service work together – which they thought about doing years before the country learned about President Barack Obama and his call for racial unity.

Chapman, a Hopkins Park resident and 32nd degree Mason tried to remain positive after the low turnout of white Masons.

Photo: Melissa Gaug
Charles Harper, Past Master 32 of St. Elmo Lodge 70A, gives the welcome address at the Brothers and Sisters United Black Tie Masonic Ball at the Quality Inn & Suites in Bradley
More photos from this shoot

"Just to see some of them show up gave me a good feeling. The word is going to get out now," Chapman said.

During the event, he spontaneously called on Bob Engstrand, a member of the Tinley Park 810 Lodge who's white, to speak. A Steger resident, Engstrand drew great applause from the crowd for "being tired of the separation," and vowing to bring some of his white Mason friends to next year's ball.

"The best way to get people to unite is to get together and have a good time," Engstrand said.

All the same

Freemasonry, a fraternal organization that arose from obscure origins in the late 16th to early 17th century, now exists in various forms all over the world. Its membership is estimated at about 5 million, with just under 2 million in the United States, according to wikipedia.org.

All Masons share moral and metaphysical ideals that include, in most cases, a constitutional declaration of belief in a Supreme Being, the Web site said.

That's why William A. Doran, who's white and a member of both St. Anne and Kankakee Masonic Lodges, didn't let heavy rain stop him from attending St. Elmo's ball.

"Whether they're black, white, green, purple, orange, red, whatever, it doesn't make any difference." Doran said. "They're brother Masons."

Doran learned about the gala when it was announced during meetings for both St. Anne and Kankakee Masonic Lodge. He told several of the members that he would attend the event, but didn't receive confirmation that any of the other members would also go. He also declined to comment about why they didn't show up.

Prior to the ball, The Daily Journal called both lodges -- as well as those in Chebanse and Peotone -- and left voice mail messages to see who would attend. No phone calls were returned in more than a week's time.

Reaching out

St. Elmo Lodge, a traditionally black Scottish Rite group first organized in 1947, has met at a small house on the north side of Kankakee since in 1956. Keeping the motto, "Making Good Men Better," the men have raised money for scholarships for local children, purchased turkeys for families at Thanksgiving, and conducted Easter egg hunts at Bird Park.

For the past three years, they have also bought Christmas gifts for second- and third-graders at Lorenzo Smith Grade School in Hopkins Park through the lodge's "Adopt-A-Class" program.

The men, however, believe that they can greater impact the community with the support of white Masons — and that their counterparts' efforts could benefit from their assistance.

The lodge, which has about 15 members, began making efforts to reach out to whites in early January. But it wasn't an easy decision.

For years, Cameron Wells, of Kankakee, said St. Elmo members were hardly ever acknowledged by white Masons while out in public locally. Even though Mason insignia would be visible on the clothing of both parties.

"They would pretend not to see you or go another direction," said Wells, a 33rd degree Mason.

Wells said he's seen some change within the past decade, however. He and his lodge brothers have been individually befriended by white Masons, particularly co-workers, although it bothers them to have learned from some of those friends that white Masons are often taught not to mingle with black Masons.

Chapman said his lodge has always embraced diversity. "As long as they're good brothers," any men can join, he said.

St. Elmo currently has two nonblack members -- Kankakee police officer Jose Martinez, who's Mexican, and John Jellema, who's white.

Jellema said race never crossed his mind when he joined the lodge three years ago. The Cedar Lake, Ind., resident called St. Elmo Lodge, "a group of fine, upstanding gentlemen" and admires their attempts to cross racial boundaries.

Said Jellema, "Right now, it's more important than ever. There's a lot that needs to be healed, and let go."

What this clandestine mason making the remark did not know was the 2009 Grand Master of the Grand Lodge of Illinois, had sent out a notice about the event stating that while he was sure it was a positive event, these Masons are not recognized by the Grand Lodge of Illinois, meaning they are clandestine.

Thursday, March 26, 2009
Clandestine Lodge - Beware
Brethren; I'm not sure if you are aware of this or not, but on March 7th there was a meeting conducted in Bradley by St. Elmos lodge #70A. There were letters sent out to some area lodges asking them to attend. Mr. Charles Harper from some Scottish rite spoke at the meeting. St. Elmos lodge is not recognized by our Grand Lodge or by the Prince Hall Grand Lodge. While there were, I'm sure, some interesting things presented, this is not approved by either Grand Lodge of Illinois. Please get the word out to all your lodges that I do not recommend attending meetings of this organization and that communications from them do not need to be read in their lodges. Please keep me informed if there is further communication with them.
Daniel C. Yandel
Grand Master[lxiii]

This was to mean that it is suggested no regular Master Mason should attend the event. That is why very few white Masons were there, it was not authorized by their regular Grand Lodge, not because they were racist. To place it in an even better perspective, the Grand Master at that time, and still to this day, personally knew my father, a Prince Hall Mason.

[lxiii] http://easternillinoisfreemasonry.blogspot.com/2009/03/clandestinelodge-

beware.html

This absence of the knowledge, or refused acceptance of the practice of the standards of recognition by the Conference of Grand Masters of Masons of North America, and the Conference of Prince Hall Grand Master of Masons of North America, of what is defined as a regular lodge by this clandestine lodge, or most of the members thereof, would have made it understandable why they could not attend. This lack of knowledge or acceptance as to the by-laws, constitution and obligation of a Regular Master Mason perpetuated the perception there was racist motives for not attending, when race had nothing to do with non-attendance at all. Having been a regular Master Mason in the jurisdiction of Illinois for three years now, in the more than 70 separate Lodges I have visited in many different states, I have never been witness to any kind of racist behavior or heard remarks intended to be racist. In fact, I have never been a part of an organization in my life where I felt more at home because no one sees race, they see men. Since my becoming a member of my Lodge and the word getting out, we have had many different ethnicities petition and successfully become members.

This is of course not to say that there is not racism practiced in the Fraternity of Freemasons. Does it happen in the more northern states of the United States? Just as the great migration of African-Americans from the South to the North could happen due to the greater prevalence of open-minded citizens, so in the Fraternity is there more open-minded Masons who by the very nature of where they live, welcome any man of good report to petition their lodges and become upright men before God and man.

There was a very public case of blatant racism in Georgia very recently. In 2009, un-masonic conduct charges were levied against the Worshipful Master of Gate City Lodge no. 2, Michael J. Bjelajac, by Worshipful Master Sterling A. Hicks, for raising to the sublime Degree of Master Mason, a non-white man, Victor Marshall. Gate City and Bjelajac, represented by members

David J. Llewellyn and C. David Johnston respectively, and then brought a Complaint in DeKalb Superior Court against the Grand Lodge of Georgia, those individuals who preferred the Masonic Charges, and the individual who agreed to chair the trial of the Charges. The Grand Master, J. Edward Jennings, Jr., On February 25, 2009, issued a statement saying, ". . . [Marshall] is a regular Mason and should be received as such,"[lxiv] after which, Gate City 2 and its Worshipful Master withdrew the charges.

Brother Victor Marshall has gone on two become Worshipful Master of Gate City Lodge no. 2, and even though initially blackballed by the Valley of Atlanta, he has also been accepted as a member and has received his Black Cap, which means his 32°. But obviously, this whole ordeal was the product of racist beliefs that are deeply held by some in the southern part of the country predominately, who tend to be products of generational remnants of a darker time in history. Logic dictates that it does exist in smaller capacities in other parts of the United States as well, and has found its way into our Fraternity even today.

[lxiv] http://www.nytimes.com/2009/07/03/us/03masons.html?_r=0

The Grand Master of Georgia did issue an edict, No. 2009-1, to clarify the position of the Grand Lodge to tenure in the state, its scope, its status in the world as a Grand Lodge of Freemasons and that it offers its privileges to men of all races, colors, and national origins who believe in a Supreme Being. It ensures that nowhere in the constitution or rituals used by the Grand Lodge of Georgia that no petitioner is to be excluded in regards to race, color, or national origin and that all constituent lodges under the jurisdiction of the Grand Lodge of Georgia Free and Accepted Masons.

The Grand Master is to be commended for this edict as it puts to rest any misinterpretations of laws from the recent past. It does give a strong indication of feelings held by members. One could interpret that the Lodges that brought forth the charges were only acting to enforce the prior Constitutional

lxv http://www.nytimes.com/2009/07/03/us/03masons.html?_r=0

Laws of the Grand Lodge. By the letter of the Grand Lodge's laws they were correct, but in the view of what is in the best interest of the Fraternity as a morally progressive institution, they were wrong to bring forth unmasonic conduct charges. It took a civil lawsuit in a public court to bring forth a morally correct change. This did not have to be though. A Masonic Lodge should be emanating morally progressive conduct to the profane world, not have the world of the profane force Freemasonry to govern themselves accordingly.

The follow up question that should be investigated by the Grand Lodge of Georgia is if there are any more cases where petitioners may have been excluded based off the original pretexts. Is there any proactive action being taken to encourage different ethnicities to feel welcomed in petitioning a Georgia Grand Lodge? Is Gate City Lodge no. 2 the only Lodge with more than one African-American that reflects the community, or are there more examples? If there are, it should be made more public to quell speculation on continued practices of exclusion. Not to only place the hones on the Grand Lodge of Georgia, why hasn't the Prince Hall Grand Lodge of Georgia responded with words of support for Grand Master Jennings forward thinking edict. They are regarded as clandestine by Georgia, but this can be a gesture to bring the gap. If the United Grand Lodge of England can regard Co-Masonic Lodges as clandestine, but still communicate with them, why cannot this be done in Georgia?

The Grand Lodge

of Free and Accepted Masons for the State of Georgia

J. Edward Jennings, Jr.
Grand Master

211 Hazel Drive
Dalton, GA 30721
(H) 706-259-8832
jej2009wgm@yahoo.com

August 19, 2009

EDICT No. 2009-1

TO ALL CONSTITUTENT LODGES UNDER THE CONSTITUTION OF THE GRAND LODGE OF GEORGIA, FREE & ACCEPTED MASONS:

WHEREAS: Freemasonry has existed in Georgia since it founding in 1734 and is the oldest Fraternal organization in the State, and;

WHEREAS: Freemasonry is universal in scope, being a Brotherhood of Man under the Fatherhood of God, and;

WHEREAS: the Grand Lodge of Georgia, Free & Accepted Masons, holds membership in this worldwide Brotherhood, and;

WHEREAS: our Ancient and Honorable Fraternity welcomes to its doors and offers its privileges to men of all races, colors and national origins who believe in a Supreme Being, as stated in our Degrees and Lectures, and;

WHEREAS: no reference is made to exclude any petitioner with regard to race, color or national origin in any of the Rituals or Masonic Code authorized for use in the Constituent Lodges chartered by the Grand Lodge of Georgia, Free and Accepted Masons, and;

WHEREAS: it is incumbent on all members of our Brotherhood to abide by the Rules, Regulations, Laws and Edicts of the Grand Lodge of Georgia, Free and Accepted Masons;

So, are the problems we seem to hear about from time to time in the Fraternity a result of cultural differences or racism? The answer is both. The lodge is a microcosm of the society and thus, the attitudes of the community can be found existing in the minds of Lodge members, to an extent. A lack of education about the fraternal relationships between Grand Lodges, mainstream and Prince Hall Affiliated Grand Lodges promotes separatism that should not exist. A Mason made a statement that exemplifies some of the knowledge of Brethren in some states where this recognition exists.

"Moorish masons are nothing more than clandestine masons. In many states including Illinois.,(Obama state) Prince hall masons are also considered clandestine and very few REAL Freemasons have any respect for them. Illinois has several PHA Grand lodges, and all of them are clandestine!!! They are NOT capable of behaving and/or conducting themselves as true freemasons and every time an argument starts, a bunch of them go start a new Grand Lodge. My statement is true and is NOT about race or racism, so don't pull out your "race card" on me.....you will not like where I stick it!!! It is a matter of CHARACTER and mental capacity.., as well as the fact that one cannot teach the unteachable."[lxvi]

In this statement, the gentleman makes clear that he is not a racist, however his demonstration of the lack of informed education as to the amity that exists between the Grand Lodge of Illinois and the Prince Hall Grand Lodge of Illinois perpetuates separation between the bodies. How many Brethren is he teaching this information too? What is the domino effect of inaccurate beliefs such as this?

There should be no contention that the results of slavery, the Civil War, the Great Migration to the north, Jim Crow Laws of the south, the Civil Rights Movement, and many other events that fall before, after and in between these major events, have not left its scare upon the culture of the United States.

[lxvi] http://www.facebook.com/photo.php?fbid=187939354690868&seta.14

3150659169738.33013.14274495243642&type=1&theater

White men who are not racist tend to be seen being pro-active in speaking politically correct in fear that they may say something perceived as racist. African-Americans are overly cautious because of the many injustices done to them by other citizens and the government of the United States for centuries gone past. This results in a terrible cycle of mistrust. So, when there is change in how men are treated, it is not noticed. When there isn't change in the mindset of men about those of the opposite race, it perpetuates the generational feeling of racism that has no place in reasonable mind with the understanding of logic. The cure for these feelings is the adherence to Masonic tenets and obligations and a complete understanding of the philosophy found within our rituals and lectures.

When a man is sitting outside of the preparation room door, we as Masons, must be sure that whatever prejudices this candidate may have had are left outside the Lodge doors to vanish forever, never seeing the inside of a Masonic Lodge. Fear in new learning of a higher level of morality must be replaced with trust of a deeper understanding of man's purpose. The teaching of living within due bounds of all mankind must be shown, and not assumed to be known exactly what "all mankind" encompasses. Everything means all. One must then ensure that the candidate understands the moral responsibility he has taken upon himself, for he will find himself in one situation or another where the principles of our honorable fraternity will be measured against the sentiments of an old society filled with animosity, hate, bigotry, and immoral beliefs, and that Brother must remember in whom he placed his trust.

To be a Freemason is not for the weak-minded or hatred filled man. It is not for those who fear taking a stance against those things which will cause a regression in societal norms or moral standing instead of a progression. It is not for those that do not place opinions of what is right through the filter of logic and rational thinking and then measure the results against the divine moral law of the volume of sacred law.

Throughout history, in every society where tyranny has stood, it was a Freemason who would not yield. Every war against oppression, a Freemason was present to push back. In the absence of knowledge, a Freemason was present to say, "Here is knowledge, here is the light to see it, now freely learn." From King Solomon's Temple to Charles the Great's decision to hire Alcuin to be the architect of the rebuilding of York, the Knights Templar crusades, the French and American Revolution, the abolishment of slavery, World War I and II, the civil rights movement, yes, Masons were present and led the way to a better existence for humanity.

Between the past and the present, times and laws have changed, most for the better, but the laws and values of our Institution have been stable. They have been constant and have survived for centuries, both in unrecorded history passed from mouth-to-ear, and recorded history. Masons from operative to speculative have been progressive builders. We went from building physical structures to spiritual structures, all the while we have building men and equipping them with the tools to journey as traveling men who would succeed in foreign countries, earning their honest wages. I ask you, are you still working in the quarry, honestly earning your wages? Are you a member, or are you a Freemason? I leave it for your conscience to decide, for it is the thoughts of a man, and the spirit in his heart, that the Supreme Architect of the Universe will ultimately see, and it is he who will judge when we have parted from our earthly remains.

A Possible Answer

What is the answer to all the negativity that hides in the darkness where the light of truth sometimes finds it difficult to exert its rays? We all must take more responsibility in being Master Masons. The day of a Mason's raising to the sublime degree of Master Mason is a powerful one. The Brother does know exactly what to make of the experience of which he has just taken part, but he knows that it was special and centuries old. Though it took hours to complete, most of it went by in a blur. He knows a bunch of ritual was spoken. When he could see clearly, he listened to many lectures recited to him from the memory of Master Masons. Marveled at how men could have so much secured in their memories, reciting paragraph after paragraph, new Master Masons generally stand in shock. Men giving lectures, seemingly as if they were just talking instead of delivering them verbatim, shock and awe after the incredible words that describe so much moral beauty would most likely describe the thoughts in their minds instead of the understanding of what they are being told are their new life long responsibilities.

As I read remarks written on public forums on the internet by Masons from around the world, my heart tends to glow with the warmth at the thought that men, only strangers by name, share the same ideas of a world-wide brotherhood, reciting statements that mainly only other regular Masons would recognize. Now, until one Masons has either sat in a Lodge with a Brother, or confirmed his membership, he cannot truly know if men speaking on some of these sites are Masons, but because the internet is not secure and no "secret" information is exchanged, it is harmless fun and fellowship. Or, is it?

I was recently reading a comment on a site used by the public with many posters, supposed Master Masons, excitedly sharing photos of the Lodge in which they hold membership and displaying their love for the Craft. Masons proudly showed pictures of their Lodge rooms and of their members. Other

Masons remarked at their displeasure of certain Grand Lodge recognition issues that plague our Fraternity, and at times, has existed long before freemasonry broached the shores of the United States. None of this is shocking to hear as the internet has provided a wonderful new avenue for Masons to communicate about issues that affect the Fraternity. What was a cause for concern is the amount of misinformation held by Brethren about things that are not left up to speculation?

One man, claiming to be a Mason, repeatedly remarked after seeing a picture of two Masons of different races standing together, "There is something incredibly wrong with this picture." It seems he was insinuating that two men of different races should not be pictured together as Masons. Another troubling comment was towards the issue of the southern Grand Lodges and the southern Prince Hall Grand Lodges status of and absence of a formal recognition agreement. Another Masons made remarks about the Grand Lodge of Florida and the expulsion of a Mason for not being of an acceptable religion that is compatible with the requirements of a belief in the "type" of Supreme Being. Another Mason supported the expulsion of such religious types stating they "those types of people, do not belong in Freemasonry.

Personally, I support a man's informed conclusion about any topic that takes into consideration a balanced sense of logic, and one that is reflective, in one way or the other, of the facts surrounding any conflicting topic. Philosophers call these types of debates scientific arguments. Each person brings to the arena of disagreement an unemotional fact that can be for, or against, certain standards relating to an issue. The problem is that sometimes these facts bring with them feelings that can tend to cloud the logical process of a calm debate.

What is troubling is that, what I have seen publically in these several forums, is reflective of what tends to be at the root of some of the troubles with the communication that tends to exist in and amongst Masons. One Brother with an absolutist opinion about an issue and hold it beyond contention, the other Brother can be just as steadfast against his Brother's opinion. Notice I said opinion and not a conclusion of facts. My concern is: Why is this happening more and more and, could it be a deteriorating issue affecting the Craft? It is very easy for one to say to another, "Remember your Obligation Brother," attempting to give a Brother a moment of pause before his actions become regrettable. I wonder how many truly understand their obligation beyond the ability to recite it from memory.

This lack of understanding of the context of our ritual is probably not limited to the obligation. How many times have you heard one say, "Remember your charge, my Brother?" How many times while memorizing the ritual and lectures do we look up that word we have never seen or pronounced before to see what it means in the context it is said, and how exactly is it even pronounced? I had a discussion not too long ago, and I just happen to like to use words I learn in ritual in regular conversations, I injected a word as it specifically conveyed exactly what I meant. The Past Master, who had sat in the Oriental Chair previous times, was insulted by the word I used saying that I was talking over him with the large words I was using.

I apologized to the Brother as I did not use the word to insult his intelligence. I also did not have the heart to tell him the word comes right out of the ritual we tell candidates in our degrees. In that moment, it was becoming clear to me the extent of which we were holding ourselves responsible to the commitment we all had taken, which does not stop at being explained to us at the end of the obligation. Our responsibilities had been explained to us when we were first received into a Lodge of Masons and extends through the charge to the Master

Mason at the end of the Third degree. How many listen, though? I mean, truly listen, and understand?

When a man is raised to the Sublime Degree of Master Mason, the Lodge is announcing to the world that this man has be proven to have mastered the knowledge of his Craft, the same as when one is a master of his craft in the operative days, his knowledge has been certified by the master of which he had apprenticed. How many Masters are certain that when a man is made a Master Builder, he has truly mastered, or another word to use here, understood completely his responsibility of being called a Master.

Now, being a Master does not mean one is "all knowing," for only the one which we each, individually refer to as our Deity, possess that absolute title. But, we should have a somewhat complete understanding of those things for which we have obliged ourselves. A man taking a vow of marriage obliges to certain things. For the sake of being religiously neutral, I will quote a civil wedding vow:

> I take you to be my lawfully wedded (husband/wife).
> Before these witnesses, I vow to love you and care for you
> As long as we both shall live.
> I take you, with all your faults and strengths,
> As I offer myself to you
> With all my faults and strengths.
> I will help you when you need help, and
> Turn to you when I need help.
> I choose you as the person with whom I will spend my life.[lxvii]

[lxvii] http://www.figstreet.com/guesthouse/simpleweddingceremony.html

#Simple

Now, these vows are very specific. One is avowing to take of the other, in good times and bad, for better or worse, till deaths do they part. This means that no matter what, they vow to be with one another, forsaking all others and disparages, until their death. Most people understand these vows, even if 50% of couples now-a-days end up in divorce because they do not possess the ability to keep these vows due to commitment issues or selfishness, or even immaturity. They said them and then they forget they swore to keep them. Did they understand what they were committing themselves too in the first place?

Let us go back to some of the examples I previously listed as the topics of arguments on some of these forums, like I said, they happen to be some of the same arguments happening outside of the internet. But, before we analyze the "what" of these arguments, let us explore the "why" of how these arguments come to be in existence in the first place. It must do with the reception and analyzing of information a man processes. How does one gain knowledge in the first place, especially about the plethora of ideas and facts presented in the fraternity.

Philosophy is a good place to start. In the study of philosophy, one learns how to disseminate between what is knowledge and what is common sense. Philosophers refer to this kind of examination as epistemology. "Epistemology, or the study of knowledge, investigates what we know, how we know it, and what kind of confidence we can have in our knowledge claims."

One type of knowledge is called propositional knowledge. This is where one asserts a fact of some sort, but does not substantiate the fact with scientific facts. The sky is blue is a known sort of fact. One could analyze further that the sky is blue, but it is also composed of red, orange, yellow, green, indigo and violet. Blue just happens to be the color that is most perceived by our visual capabilities. It is true the sky is blue, but it is also all the other colors. When giving the statement that the sky is blue, one does not intentionally leave out the rest of the colors, he just does not know because it is beyond his scope of knowledge. This type of knowledge can progress to analytic knowledge, or basically a deeper study weighing observations and perceptions against concrete evidence until it cannot be disproved.

Another type of knowledge is procedural knowledge. Rather than speculate on how something might be done, one has first knowledge of how it is done because they have been instructed in the discipline. For example, one knows how to change a tire, not by seeing it done, but having learned and done it personally. This person can give you step by step directions because the process is explained by first-hand knowledge.

Knowledge by association is another type of knowledge one may possess. A person asserts their knowledge by being simply associated with someone who may know something. For example, one may convey about how to do an exercise properly because they know a trainer who teaches people how to exercise. For our purposes in Freemasonry, one may assert some by-laws because he has heard his lodge Brother states some. But in fact, he does not know the by-laws himself.

These types of knowledge must be confronted with what keeps logic factual and not speculated. It must withstand scrutiny or skepticism. Skepticism is the confrontation of a stated fact to see if it withstands logical examination of credibility. It is what separates what we may believe with what is concretely known and can be proven. For example, I can think my car is the fastest in town and I can even say that I believe my car is the fastest in town, but until I race my car against every car in town, I cannot know for certain that my car is the fastest.

As a Freemason, this is what separates Brethren from obtaining enlightenment and those who simply exist without knowing what truths may exist beyond their scope. It is the difference between conceiving the intent of our rituals versus the reading and reciting of the ritual and believing that the deliverance is the extent of the learning. I have heard it said that there are parrot Masons and then there are teachers of the mystic knowledge of the Craft. A parrot will recite the ritual verbatim and when you ask what something means, they recite a sentence of the ritual. Then, there are the teachers. When a Brother asks what a certain part of the ritual is meant to convey, they give the actual incite of the words and how they relate to each of us on an individual basis. Remember, the journey of enlightenment in Freemasonry is an individual journey, to each Brother. Everyone can be shown the door and given the key, but only those who are truly desiring the proper journey can turn the key and enter. Some spend their entire Masonic careers on the front porch, all the time believing they were on the inside by the fire.

What is secret about Freemasonry and what is not secret? A Brother swore to me that sharing a picture of the inside of a Lodge room while the Lodge is closed is violating one's masonic obligation. Why did he believe with such conviction that this was exposing the secrets of Freemasonry? Has he not ever been to a Lodge Officer's public installation? Has he not been to a Grand Lodge Communication before Grand Lodge is opened while all the different woman's orders are being praised for their good work? No, he hadn't. His knowledge was limited because he did not know the facts of his Grand Lodge's constitution and By-laws, rules and regulations. He only knew what he perceived as fact without investigation or the analyzing if he was right or wrong in his assertion. It just so happens that his own Grand Lodge had a picture of all the Grand Officers in a Lodge, standing right behind a closed altar. Is the belief he is taught in his lodge correct though his Grand Lodge states differently? The answer is no.

Why some things are kept secret from the uninitiated? Certain things, such as our signs, grips, passwords and the ritual itself are kept secret. Why? They are secret because the context in which they are conveyed brings understanding. Without having been properly initiated into the Craft, one cannot understand in the proper context the information and truth he is to assimilate into his conscious and subconscious thoughts. This is the reason that anti-masonic conspiracy theorist has so much ability to draw attention to their rants, they use exposés to promote their cause and see logic in what they saw because they are uninitiated. They cannot understand the ritual in the proper context as they are simply reading and deciphering rather than going through the ritual itself. They see our signs, symbols and such in a way that only the uninitiated or even the misinformed Mason himself can see them. Again, this is knowledge learned through association. They think they know because they see what they choose to see, but they do not know the how because they do not have hands-on experience.

How does a Brother learn than what is secret and what is not? Simple, review the obligation and then seek out more Brethren to discuss what every part of the obligation means and in the context that it is meant. Also, seek out the Grand Lodge's position of what can be shown to the public and what is not. Then, we must individually compare what we have been told from the different sources with certain logic. Logic is specifically a science that deals with the principles and criteria of validity of inference and demonstration. As the Entered Apprentice degree prepares our heart, which is the seat of our conscience, the Fellowcraft degrees prepares our mind to assimilate ideas and differentiate between what is opinion and what simply "is." This is done to draw a proper and beneficial conclusion that does not necessarily promote our own interest, but one that benefits all worthy Brother Master Masons. This is a reflective process that emanates goodness out to the world.

When we say that we are obliged not to expose the secrets of Freemasonry, we are referring to all those things that are done in a tyled Lodge. Is a Lodge tyled when it is closed? No, it is not. Is the altar still present when a Lodge is closed? Yes, it is. So, seeing the lodge room while the lodge is not tyled is not exposing a secret. Again, there is a presumption of what is secret and there is logical deduction of what is secret. One should not have to be told a lodge room presents no secrets if he surmises that a lodge is always tyled when it is open. No Tyler, no open lodge, no secrets to protect.

How about recognition between Grand Lodges and appendant bodies? A Brother remarked that the Grand Lodge of Tennessee does not recognize the Most Worshipful Prince Hall Grand Lodge of Tennessee because the Prince Hall Grand Lodge does not pay their per capita tax to the Grand Lodge of Tennessee. Why would they? Both Grand Lodges are sovereign onto themselves and both Grand Lodges are regular in their forming. I asked the Brother if he had ever heard of the Exclusive Territorial Jurisdiction Doctrine. He said, "No." Now, not everybody knows what ETJ is, but doesn't it seem strange that one Grand Lodge would pay another Grand Lodge per capita in the same respect a subordinate Lodge pays per capita for each of their members?

Another subject that is brought up whenever there is a conversation relating to the recognition between Grand Lodges and Prince Hall Grand Lodges is that all Grand Lodges in the south do not desire to extend recognition to Prince Hall Grand Lodges out of racism as these Grand Lodges are the Confederate States of the Civil War era. This is simply not true. One cannot concede all Grand Lodges do not want recognition with Prince Hall Grand Lodges. The Grand Lodge of Texas extended recognition to the Prince Hall Grand Lodge of Texas. However, the Prince Hall Grand Lodge of Texas did not want visitation.

Section III of the Compact agreement between the Grand Lodge of Texas and the Most Worshipful Grand Lodge of Texas states:

"Be it remembered that on December 1, 2006, The Most Worshipful Grand Lodge of Texas, in its 171st Grand Annual Communication acted favorably on the July 13, 2005, request of The Most Worshipful Prince Hall Grand Lodge of Texas, F. & A. M., and Jurisdiction, requesting fraternal recognition, which said request in no way is a request to join, merge, meet, interfere or have visitation between the two jurisdictions and that it is only for the two Grand Lodges to acknowledge and formally recognize each other as being legitimate and regular."[lxviii]

[lxviii] Compact between the Most Worshipful Grand Lodge of Texas and

the Most Worshipful Prince Hall Grand Lodge

Of Texas and Jurisdiction, F. & A.M., signed April 23, 2007 Donny W.

Broughton and Wilbert M. Curtis, Grand

Masters of both Grand Lodges, respectively.

Texas Grand Lodges Sign Compact to Share Territorial Rights
April 23, 2007

Board of Trustees and Compact Committee Members of the two Grand Lodges

Compact Between
The Grand Lodge of Texas, A.F. & A.M.
and
The Prince Hall Grand lodge of Texas, F. & A.M.
To Share Territorial Rights within the State of Texas

On June 18, 2005, The Prince Hall Grand Lodge of Texas at its 130th Grand Communication voted to request mutual fraternal recognition with The Grand Lodge of Texas. The request dated July 13, 2005 was submitted to The Grand Lodge of Texas.

On December 1, 2006, The Grand Lodge of Texas in its 171st Grand Annual Communications acted favorably on the July 13, 2005, request by The Prince Hall Grand Lodge of Texas for fraternal recognition, noting that the request in no way was a request to join, merge, interfere, or have visitation between the two jurisdictions. It was only for the two Grand Jurisdictions to acknowledge and formally recognize each other as being legitimate and regular.

Also acted upon favorably in December 2006 was the report of the Fraternal Relations Committee and its recommendation that the two jurisdictions enter into a treaty of mutual consent for sharing territorial jurisdiction within the State of Texas.

On April 23, 2007, the Trustees and a Special Committee of both Grand Jurisdictions met and completed a Compact to Share Territorial Rights. By mutual consent these two Grand Jurisdictions (Grand Lodge of Texas that was formed in 1837 and Prince Hall Grand Lodge of Texas that was formed in 1875) legitimized the fact that both Grand Lodges had shared the same territory since 1875.

On June 23, 2007, at the 132nd Grand Communications of the Prince Hall Grand Lodge of Texas, a resolution to ratify the Fraternal Relations Committee Report on mutual Fraternal Recognition and the Compact to Share Territorial Rights in the State of Texas will be voted on for approval.

Masons of both Grand Jurisdictions should be aware that the actions taken by their Grand Jurisdictions restricts their members from joining, visiting, merging, meeting, or having Masonic communications with each other. These actions guarantees the autonomy of each organization and assure the right to reside and work together in Peace, Harmony, and Brotherly Love.

The ultimate goal for the Prince Hall Grand Lodge of Texas is to obtain mutual Fraternal recognition with the Mother Grand Lodge, The United Grand Lodge of England. This is the first step in obtaining that goal.

Most Worshipful Donnie W. Broughton of the Grand Lodge of Texas, A.F. & A.M. and Most Worshipful Wilbert M. Curtis of the Prince Hall Grand Lodge of Texas, F. & A.M. sign Compact to share territorial rights in the State of Texas. Right Worshipful Tommy Guest, Grand Secretary of the Grand Lodge of Texas, A.F. & A.M. looks on.

Prince Hall Grand Lodge Officers Present:

Most Worshipful Wilbert M. Curtis	Grand Master
Right Worshipful Michael T. Anderson	Deputy Grand Master
Right Worshipful Willie High Coleman, Jr.	Grand Senior Warden Committee Chairman
Right Worshipful Norris Jackson	Grand Junior Warden
Right Worshipful Hubert L. Reece	Grand Secretary
Worshipful Frank Jackson	Grand Historian

Grand Lodges are sovereign and it is not up to anyone to try to infer why a Grand Lodge does, or does not, want visitation. However, there are many uninformed men who simply think Texas did not want Prince Hall Masons in their Lodge because of race. While no one should assume to guess, what is in a man's mind, the stipulations of this compact shows that it was the Prince Hall Grand Lodge that did not desire mutual visitation at the time of this compact. Again, another example of speculated truth and the facts of what truly exists. This similar compact also exists between the Grand Lodge of Kentucky and the Most Worshipful Grand Lodge of Kentucky. The question should be asked, "What is the point of recognition without visitation?"

Establishment of the recognition between Texas and the Prince Hall Grand Lodge of Texas, and that of Kentucky and the Prince Hall Grand Lodge of Kentucky can be said that it is progress. But, is it true progress, or politically correct progress? What is the point of mutually recognizing one another if you cannot sit in Lodge together and share the benefit of different practices of Freemasonry to expand one's knowledge? An individual that is aware of the civil rights issues extending from before the civil war, and through to 1963, should instantly recognize this as "Separate, but equal." We can call each other the same thing, but we cannot act together as if we are the same. We can both drink water from the water fountain, but we cannot drink the same water from the same fountain.

The problem is the lack of understanding of what we are here to do. We say the usual standard statements of, "We take good men and make them better," or "We come here to subdue are passions and improve ourselves in being a Mason." The question is, how? How are we improving ourselves if we do not even understand all the words in the several lines of masonic catechism to deliver our proficiencies? Further than that, how are we Masters of our Craft and exercising our rights to explore Masonic communication when we have not learned what the trivium and quadrivium means to how we process thought and convey meaningful messages? How are we showing we are leaders of a morally progressive society when our public examples dictate the opposite?

It is through the understanding of the lectures that we can more efficiently execute our purpose in life within the bounds of our obligation. How can we correct the irregularities of our less informed Brothers when we ourselves do not have a clear understanding of what Masonic irregularities even are? How can we subdue our passions when we have not analyzed what our vices are in comparison to our own divine moral law? How can we change from who we were to who we are going to be if, as Brother John S. Nagy, author of Building Better Builders, the acclaimed Masonic Education book series, often says, "When we have not done the work of each degree?"

Too many arguments happen that get incredibly out of proportion due to Masons who are Masters, but have not mastered what they have obliged to master, if that makes sense. If I am to act within due bounds of all mankind, don't I need to subdue preconceived notions of the parts of humanity I previously held prejudices against? If I am to understand the logic another is using, don't I need to first understand what logic is and how to define the credibility that establishes the foundation of one's logic? If I am to subdue my passion, shouldn't I learn how to accept criticism and carry a sense of humility? Otherwise, how do we ever keep adding to our knowledge if we believe we know everything already?

Socrates said, "As for me, all I know is that I know nothing." Socrates, the philosopher that lived in the 500 BCE eras, who taught philosophy to Plato, is considered one of the first great thinkers. So, why would one of the greatest philosophers of all time say a line like this? He said this because his idea of knowledge was always held beyond what he already knew. If he knew everything, he would have never had a question to ask. He knew that if a man ever reached the point that he did not retain humility in thought as one of his greatest attributes; his ability to learn would cease, and therefore negate his advancement in personal growth.

We must all take a page from Socrates. It is not that there are not many wise men in and outside of our Craft, quite the opposite. However, no of us are so intelligent, or knowledgeable, to assume that we know all there is to know about everything. There is always knowledge that exists right beyond our present comprehension. If we accept this, perhaps one would not be so quick to dismiss another's proposal. Perhaps, it would be easier to spread the cement of brotherly love over the cracks that exist amongst our order since none of us are perfect. Perfection cannot be obtained, but work is required to become better. All men are in the transition between the rough and the perfect ashlar.

Perhaps in the next confrontation of our proposal, we might remember that no one can afford to be absolute in their thinking. For if we are all to meet on the level, then we are all equal in our imperfections and hopefully, all aspire to learn more about each other, and ourselves. Remember my Brethren, it takes materials such as cement, clay, sand, iron ore and limestone, brought together in a proper manner to make cement. No one part alone can make cement, it takes all kinds. We, as Masonic Brethren, also are made up of all kinds. Brought together properly, we make the cement that unites us into one common mass, which is the intent of Fraternal Brotherhood. From one mix of different materials...

To another...

Both making strong cement, spread properly, uniting all components into one common mass for strength and support for the future to build upon.

Thus, we can truly show to the world the Universality of man under the Fatherhood of the Supreme Architect of the Universe, and truly unite humankind.

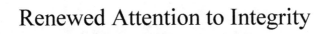

Renewed Attention to Integrity

Integrity is defined by the Merriam-Webster dictionary as the "firm adherence to a code of especially moral or artistic values."[lxix] For society in general, it is common place to believe that most families and individuals define their morals relative to their culture, which mostly includes a specific religion. A conclusion can be drawn that one's moral commitment is relevant to the understanding of the proper interpretation of their faith in its application to produce an expected behavior. The firm adherence to this code or belief derives one's integrity.

When one studies integrity and what it is composed of, the direction they are lead to learn about is ethics and its several applications in life. Ethics tends to be an area of study that is not necessarily popular, but it is in everyday use, whether one is aware of it or not, its use is imperative to positive progressive relationships. Ethics is the moral guide that one depends on to derive a decision on whether something is good or bad, and right or wrong. The study of ethics explains WHY something is good or bad, and right or wrong.

[lxix] http://www.merriam-webster.com/dictionary/integrity

Most of the great debates in general society are ones of ethics, and in which many people tend to be emotionally connected too, and in which most cases it means that they are extremely passionate about these topics. Abortion, gay marriage, woman in combat, and others, tend to draw out very emotionally charged debates that tend not to get resolved because the arguments that may start out as scientific debates, generally turn into drawn out emotional arguments. Once emotion clouds the mind, cognitive function decreases in the brain due to the chemicals that emotions produce, and it becomes virtually impossible to function with logical thoughts. Without logical thought to derive sound conclusions of ethics and the moral philosophy of one's faith, it becomes difficult to establish a clear sense of integrity.

There are several aspects of the business of the lodge, like that of a board of directors meeting of a corporation, that will have either positive or negative effects in the future progress of the institution, and it is all predicated on the integrity of the members. In Freemasonry, we vote on motions and we ballot on candidates. We practice democracy with voting, with the majority carrying the yeas or nays of the outcome. We ballot on the acceptance of a candidate to become a member of our Fraternity with the casting of our vote, which is secret. It is a vote that will never be known by anyone, for or against, of a candidate's acceptance into the institution.

It may be peculiar to the public why a ballot for the acceptance of a candidate would be secret, and the results indisputable. Freemasonry, as in all good institutions, promotes always, harmony amongst its members. Religion and politics are forbidden to be discussed in Lodge as they are topics which tend to cause a divide amongst Brethren. Knowing which way, a member has casted his ballot can also be a possible source of contention amongst Brethren, and therefore it is secret and beyond reproach.

Every member has a right to accept or deny someone into the trusted brotherhood, and each has a vote for what they believe is the betterment of the institution, free from any kind of verbal retribution. The results of the votes, or balloting, influences the direction of the lodge. In respect to how the members will vote in Lodge in regards to education, charity, degrees and community projects, also the representation of the Lodge in the community by how its members display their character in public, the individual member represents not just himself, but his lodge to all.

The integrity of the individual Mason becomes very important when it comes to the decision, and more importantly, the reason behind his decision, of what side of an issue he will vote and for who he will ballot to allow admittance into the Fraternity. A Mason should always keep in mind the he casts his vote for what he believes is in the best interest of the institution of Freemasonry, and his Lodge more specifically. Mind you, it is not for what is in his best interest, but what is in the best interest of something outside of himself. The development one has accomplished in the study of his faith, Masonic philosophy, combined with the environment and culture an individual has grown from, will comprise the overall basis for the type of integrity for which they are in possession.

In Masonic philosophy, the examination of the seven liberal arts and sciences help to guide one to a sound understanding of how to grow a balanced moral foundation that is the basis of integrity. Systematically, Masons are introduced to information that originated from many philosophers and ancient mystery schools of knowledge that compose these arts and sciences that splits into two parts, the trivium and quadrivium.

The trivium is composed of grammar, rhetoric and logic. In grammar, we use language appropriately and ensure we both speak and understand in a way that allows for the useful exchange of information. Rhetoric is as Sir Francis Bacon describes it, "The application of reason to imagination for the better moving of the will."[lxx] Logic, as Aristotle states it, is the "study of reasoning and is the basis for understanding and conveying credible information through grammar and rhetoric."[lxxi]

[lxx] http://www.stanford.edu/dept/english/courses/sites/lunsford/page

s/defs.htm

[lxxi] Micciche, L. 2004, Making a Case for Rhetorical Grammar, National

Council of Teachers of English,

https://www.csun.edu/~bashforth/305_PDF/305_PDF_Grammar/M

akingACaseForRhetoricalGrammar_Micciche.pdf

The quadrivium is the other four arts: arithmetic, geometry, music and astronomy. One might question what good is the study of the four mathematical sciences to philosophy. Their contribution is great. Mathematics in philosophy is a theoretical science which quantifies the measurements of all things abstract. As William H, Stahl says, it is the "abstract quantity which we treat by reason alone, separating it by the intellect from the material or from other nonessentials, as for example, equal, unequal, or the like."[lxxii]

[lxxii] Grant, E. 1974, A Source Book in Medieval Science, The Latin

Encyclopedists,   Harvard   University   Press

Through the useful application of these arts and sciences, there is a tangible result. The cognitive function of the mind develops a greater ability to quantify all things perceived through the five senses, to which in masonry there are symbolic reminders, and discern which information to store and which to discard. The information stored is examined further upon discussion amongst trusted friends, and is applied to various uses in conversational exchanges that perpetuates a revolving world of social improvement.

A symbol one might use to place this explanation into a simple form of context is the point within the circle. In this example, the two parallel lines will be excluded as to leave it purely philosophical without the influence of religion in any capacity. The individual in the middle of the circle is not the center of their universe. They are a receptacle of the mirrored reflection of those they surround themselves with through their numerous relationships in their lives. Humans tend to gravitate around those they share some similar interest or character trait, positive or negative.

This point within the circle in this example can be used as a measuring rod to gain insight into an individual's own character and level of integrity. As humans tend to be drawn to those with like traits and so forth they find to have in common, the point or person in the center of the circle can evaluate by the character of their associates what traits they themselves may have, and can therefore identify if they are themselves in need of some assessment.

To define one's integrity without bias in assessing themselves, one simply needs to look around and see with whom they have surrounded themselves. They should ask themselves, "Is this person exhibiting the character which may rub positively on me?" "Do I notice any behaviors of my friends that do not bother me, but may bother others?" "Why?" Upon these assessments, reflection on the strict moral code of one's personal faith comes into play. If $1 + 1$ does not equal 2, which produces a fallacy in logical deduction, you may have to reconsider your personal integrity based on your ideas of good and upright behavior and reanalyze what you came into the institution of Freemasonry to do.

Deriving one's integrity involves a sound understanding of each person's faith in the supreme being, and a firm grasp of the seven liberal arts and sciences to derive their view of the due bounds they are to circumscribe themselves within all mankind. Confucius says that "The strength of a nation derives from the integrity of the home." As Masons, we can extrapolate this to mean that a Lodge derives its strength from the integrity of its members.

So, as we sit in our next stated meeting and engage into the business of our lodges, let us consider by which we measure our decision when applying our rights and privileges of being Master Masons. Let us remember the several examples by which we have been taught to evaluate our own conduct and character. We do not sit in Lodge to impress another, or to gain any sense of establishment of power. We should remember that as we vote on whatever motion that is proposed, it is for the good of the entire Fraternity that we vote, and our lodges. When we are presented a candidate for the degrees of Freemasonry, and deciding to allow them into our personal place of honor and trust, it is our Creator that will peer into our souls, for the truth cannot be hidden from the Almighty. Let these things weigh in our seat of consciousness.

Mistakes will be made for as we are human, we will most undoubtedly error. Let it be for a lack of judgment, or unknown information that our mistakes are made. We will never have all the right answers to all the problems that we will confront. We must never forget though, the great lesson of some of the greatest masons the Fraternity has ever known, like the examples made known to us by our ritual, let our errors never be made for a lack of integrity. Men in history have lost their lives for the sake of their integrity. Let us conduct our decisions in Freemasonry with the same passion and resolve of the lessons our forefathers have taught us.

Chapter 5

Conclusion

What is to become of the Fraternity of Freemasons, specifically in America where it is presumed to be divided by race, where men who have not truly studied to become a Master of the Craft, are designated Masters? What is the potential outcome of a lack of appreciation of ancient practices that produced such powerfully insightful men whose works are revered today? Traditional Observance Lodges are a rarity. The use of the Chamber of Reflection is frowned upon.

Socially, the racial compositions of Lodges do not reflect entirely the communities they were formed in. Men are forced to choose if they want to petition a "Black" lodge or a "white" lodge when in Freemasonry, no such thing exists. Society forces these labels on the lodges seen, for they cannot hide the truth of the ethnic make-up of their membership. A friend and Brother of mine visited England and one of the first questions asked of him was why does America have racially separate Grand Lodges in every state?

It is a fact that this separation is partly perception, as there are Grand Lodges that make a considerable effort to intermingle with the other, but this is not taking place on the subordinate lodge level in the same manner. Few and far between are their exchanges of fraternal fellowship taking place between Prince Hall Affiliated Subordinate Lodges and the mainstream subordinate Lodges? The public questions why? How do we answer? With the age of the internet, it is not a secret these racial separations that exist, and clandestine lodges taking advantage of this division.

Many clandestine masons perpetuate separatism in the Fraternity by attempting to attach Speculative Freemasonry as stolen from one race, by another, have missed the empowerment and liberation received once investing themselves into the full study of the Craft. This separation also occurs when regular Masons attach religion conviction to freemasonry, excluding those who are not Christians or one that is not widely known. What purpose does the identity of a man's religion or attempting to specify the derivative of a portion of knowledge contained within the bounds of our Fraternity?

How liberating the feeling of seeing beyond ethnicity or creed in a country where every other conversation, whether it is politics, religion, population, pick anything issue, has race in it. One is no longer anchored in reflection of past horrid deeds, partially blinding them from social and moral advancements that can be made. If one carries a mindset that knowledge was stolen and that it is rightfully someone else's, there can be no circumscribing with mankind. Mankind is all inclusive, not exclusive because of ancestral transgressions generationally passed on. True Freemasons search to break the cycle of hatred, not within its emotionally damaging bounds.

Undoubtedly, education is the answer. The Fraternity is designed to educate through fellowship. Every Master Mason is asked why he became a Master Mason with the answer being to do as the operative masons had done which is to travel from lodge to lodge, expanding their knowledge by building on what they had learned, and sharing new ideas to improve the building of an edifice. Some history is grounded in facts, other history is allegorical, and both are combined in the foundation of the lessons we are to learn. When knowledge gained is not grounded with facts, and insight is not circumscribed within the compasses, growth is more representative of a weed than the acacia and it becomes impossible for virtuous men to be produced from the Lodge.

A conversation was had on a forum with a Mason from the state of Alabama regarding blacks in Lodge. Here is an excerpt of the conversation:

A Mason from Alabama: "You and I ain't brothers, you wouldn't be welcome here. I am not brothers with anyone that is Black."

My response: "Why are we not Brothers? Do not our Grand Lodges have fraternal recognition which establishes amity between our jurisdictions, thus declaring both of us regular Masons?

The membership of this Mason was found through his lodge's website to be from the state of Alabama. My Grand Lodge is Illinois. These two Grand Lodges share recognition and visitation. This Mason says that I would not be welcomed in his Lodge simply because of my ethnicity.

I then asked him: "Does your Lodge Brothers, Past Masters, District Deputy Grand Masters and Grand Master know you carry these views about the Fraternity and you not being the Masonic Brother of anybody who is black?"

He responded: "Yes, they know how I feel about it. Most of them feel the same way, they just don't voice their opinion like I do. At least I am tactful about it."

While I have not published the name of this Mason, this conversation is unfortunately completely true. This Mason is a Past Master, not even 40 years of age yet. He went on tell me that Prince Hall Masons are not allowed into lodges of his friends in the northern states of the country where a compact of amity exists between the states two Grand Lodges. Some might suggest that this incident is not indicative of many Masons, but the fact that it exists publicly on a regular basis and is indicative of what exists privately. The fact that it exists in any capacity at all is an issue. This however, is not an isolated issue. It happened every time there was a posting showing unity between ethnicities, specifically black and white.

On a Facebook posting, the same attitude is displayed.

May 2, 2013

Facebook

https://www.facebook.com/photo.php?fbid=186909778127159&set=a.143150659169738.33013.142744952543642&type=1&theater

Free Masonry
16 hours ago

Lorenzo Champion Walter I'm n Memphis n it's the same here Robert tell me why not
Like · Reply · 1 · 16 hours ago via mobile

Robert Williams Because some of us like things Just the way they are. It keeps peace that way
Like · 14 hours ago

Free Masonry Has there been episodes inside the Lodge where the existence of more than one race has caused disharmony to make you reach the conclusion that it would be keeping the peace the way it is?
Like · 1 · 14 hours ago

Lorenzo Champion Not trying to make a race issue or say anything negative about a brother but I've been call the n word time n time again to the point where I took my light off my truck.

Like · Reply · 16 hours ago

Derrick Robertson Racism is utterly intolerable in our lodges here in Maine as it should be. Our black past masters are equally honorable men and very well respected.
Like · Reply · 1 · 3 hours ago via mobile

Neal Lovins I don't think the South needs changing.
Like · 12 hours ago

Anthony Spraggins This will never occur in the South.......ever
Like · Reply · 1 ·

1 of 7

Albert Hamm Never
Like · Reply · via mobile

Free Masonry Why never?
Like · 10 hours ago

Robert Williams Its the fact that if blacks were in the lodge that it would cause disharmony due to the lodge being against it.
Like · Reply ·

Free Masonry What Masonic Lodge would be against it? Is there a rule that forbids the denial of a candidate based on ethnicity?
Like · 10 hours ago

Bro Harper Freemason Robert Williams, how do you know it is a fact that if blacks were in lodge that it would cause disharmony? Have you ever been in Lodge with Blacks to see this to be true? Also, is this something you are proud to support as well as your lodge? If so, please share what Lodge you hold membership? Thank you.
Like · 2 · 10 hours ago

Robert Williams Won't' never happen
Like · Reply ·
Free Masonry Robert Williams, where are you from and why do you believe this will never happen?
Walter Lynn I Wished this was True, But not in West Ky.
Like · Reply · via mobile
Robert Williams We are not all brothers

What is the answer to this dilemma? Some would say that this is a private matter to be had behind closed doors. Maybe the Grand Master should give an edict that prevents Masons from speaking on public forums to be used as evidence of such negativity in the Fraternity. This demonstration of character has existed for hundreds of years behind closed doors without progression. Preventing public discussion will not solve the bigger problem, expulsions of Masons who demonstrate such convictions is the answer.

The only reason this exists in the fraternity at all is the choice Brethren make to exclude the entire context of masonic education. If one truly studies and applies all the education Freemasonry offers, no such abundance of separation could exist. There are always individuals who slip past the investigation committee into a Lodge, but the screening process when equipped with intolerance for prejudicial attitudes, would greatly reduce these men from admittance.

This book alone will not solve anything no matter how passionate a plea is made. It is hoped that conversations being had will become effort, and not just side chatter, of what should become of our fraternity. Every Grand Lodge is sovereign and can hold whatever policies they choose, but instead of using recognition for posturing rules of appendant bodies, use it to force true adherence to Freemasonry as it is the universality of ALL men under the fatherhood of God.

Men throughout history have paid the ultimate price to maintain their integrity, as each Master Mason is taught the same lesson. We are taught responsibility of education and a strict adherence to the moral law. The social problem of the fraternity can be solved through masonic education and spreading liberally the cement of Brotherly Love. We must be of one accord and stand firm against any adherence to prejudicial beliefs of one's race or creed. We are the examples of conformity to higher moral standards. We are the progressive society that has influenced the advancement of humanity through our collective efforts for centuries. Nothing has changed in the content of our rituals. Only society has changed. We must return to our ancient practices, the place whence we came if we are to be, and produce, the moral leaders of tomorrow.

In his Faith, my Brethren, look well to the East. The answers are directly in front of us and we only need the courage to adhere and stand for them. As the Grand Lodge of Illinois asks, "Who are you going to be?" I will add the question, "When do we begin?"

Acknowledgments

I give praise to the Supreme Grand Architect of the Universe, my Deity, for blessing me with the ability to learn to convey my thoughts and gaining the courage to find the direction of my ultimate charity towards mankind. To my parents, thank you for your patience in raising such a defiant child. It was only a matter of time until I found purpose to compliment my nature. Thank you Right Worshipful Brother Robert Herd for giving me the opportunity to write for the Living Stones Magazine and honing my skills as a writer with a large masonic platform. To Brother John S. Nagy, thank you for showing me how to examine Masonry as opposed to simply being a Freemason. Worshipful Brother Cliff Porter, thank you for being my mentor in publishing my book. To Worshipful Brother Andrew Hammer, your inspiration to be more observant of the Craft continues to move a generation of Masons to seek more out of Freemasonry. Brother Robert Johnson of the "Whence You Came" masonic podcast, thank you for granting my first interview to share my insights. To my Masonic Brethren who traveled with me on my various learning trips, Brother Shaun McPhail, Jammie Shell, Emmett George, Leon Sullivan and many others, your friendship is immeasurable. To the 2013-2014 Worshipful Master of Pleiades Lodge No. 478, Brother Stephen Valle, your support is immeasurable. To Right Worshipful Brother Mir Omar Ali, thank you greatly for your contribution to this book. Your encouragement of me to speak to the masses about those things needing attention, which can truly be a daunting and worrisome task, gave me the motivation I needed to complete this book. To the many friends that have contributed to my educational journey in so many facets, thank you.

Charles M. Harper Sr. has a Bachelor's Degree in Liberal Arts and Sciences, and a minor in Cultural Anthropological Studies. He is an educator of U.S. History. As a published author of three books, having made appearances on talk radio shows about racial prejudice, a featured writer for the Living Stones Magazine, including being the writer and star of the inspiring play Black and White: A Man Divided which features and is produced by 5-Time Grammy Award Winner Malik Yusef, I bring academics and entertainment together to inspire considerations for moral change.

Bibliography

i http://www.msana.com/focusarchives/focusapr01.asp

ii This photo was taken by Brother Jammie Shell, a member of Kankakee Lodge No. 389, in Portsmouth, Ohio, during the Black Watch tour of the Grand Lodge of Scotland.

iii http://www.merriam-webster.com/dictionary/mulatto

iv Jandt, F. 2013. An Introduction to Intercultural Communication: Identities in a Global Community. Sage Publications, Inc.

v http://www.irishmasons.com.sg/concf/index.php/history

vi A Cairo Masonic lodge in the 1940s, under a portrait of King Farouk

vii http://www.lulu.com/shop/albert-pike-and-foreword-by-michaelr-poll/morals-and-dogma-of-the-scottish-ritecraftdegrees/paperback/product-1211287.html

viii http://music-row.ru/blog/rick_ross_free_mason/2010-08-08-993

ix http://www.strictlyfitteds.com/blog/2011/04/rocawear%E3%80%8C wool%E3%80%8Dfitted-baseball-cap

x Mackey, A. 1873, Encyclopedia of Freemasonry, Moss and co. pg. 800

xi http://legende-hiram.blogspot.com/2010/07/blog-post_22.html

xii Stauffer, V., The European Illuminati, http://freemasonry.bcy.ca/anti-masonry/stauffer.html

xiii Mackey, A. 1873, Encyclopedia of Freemasonry, Moss and co. pg. 800

xiv http://ioof.org/aboutus.html

xv http://www.phoenixmasonry.org/masonicmuseum/goat_riding_tricy cle.htm

xvi http://www.freemason.org/discoverMasonry/qa.htm#twelve

xvii Regius Manuscript, on or about 1390

xviii Anderson, J. The Constitutions of the Free-Masons, 1734Pg. 53 Article 2

xix Anderson, J. Pg. 51

xx http://www.merriam-webster.com/dictionary/inspiration

xxi http://www.ncdc.noaa.gov/special-reports/katrina.html

xxii http://supremecouncil.org/rss/February2012/201202-04.htm

xxiii www.livingstonesmagazine.com advertisement

xxiv Gest, K. 2011, The Mandorla and Tau, Lewis Masonic, pg. 79 The quote is from the book The Story of the City Companies by P.H. Ditchfield MA FSA, and he is quoting Edward III monarch 1327-1377

xxv http://www.mastermason.com/wnymasons/Silver_Lodge/History/History%20of%20Freemasonry_files/cantiere02.jpg

xxvi Gest, K., 2011, Mandorla and Tau, pg. 84

xxvii Tabbert, M. 2005, American Freemason: Three Centuries of Building Communities, New York University Press;

Alvin J. Schmidt, 1980, Fraternal Organizations, Greenwood Press

xxviii http://www.docs.is.ed.ac.uk/docs/libarchive/ bgallery/Gallery/records/eighteen/halliwell.html

xxix Regius Manuscript, 1390 appox.

xxx Anderson, J. 1834, The Constitutions of Free-Masons, London, pgs 50, 51

xxxi Anderson, J. pg 51

xxxii http://encyclopediaoffreemasonry.com/m/moray-sir-robert/

xxxiii http://www.historylearningsite.co.uk/great_fire_of_london_of_1666.htm

xxxiv William Preston, 1867, 2012, Illustrations of Masonry, this book was originally written in 1776, two years' after

Preston was Master of the Lodge of Antiquity. Pg. 136

xxxv Preston, illustrations of Masonry, pg. 149

xxxvi http://www.ugle.org.uk/about-ugle/

xxxvii Records in the custody of the Grand Lodge of Ireland are the following: -

Transcript of Minutes covering the period 1796 to 1821.

Original in the care of the Officers' Mess, 1st Btn. South Staffordshire Regt.

xxxviii http://www.conferenceofgrandmasterspha.org/gmasters_history.asp

xxxix http://www.conferenceofgrandmasterspha.org/gmasters_history.asp

xl Evans, H., 2003, Cagliostro and his Egyptian Rite of Freemasonry, A Master of Magic, Pg. 1, Cornerstone Book

Publishers Lafayette, LA

xli http://www.moorishriteonline.net/freemasonry.htm

xlii http://internationalmasons.org/about_us.html

xliii http://internationalmasons.org/about_us.html

xliv http://internationalmasons.org/about_us.html

xlv http://internationalmasons.org/about_us.html

xlvi http://www.thephylaxis.org/phylaxis/index.php

xlvii http://codes.lp.findlaw.com/nycode/GBS/9-B/137

xlviii http://www.thephylaxis.org/phylaxis/index.php

xlix http://freemasonry.bcy.ca/grandlodge/trademark.html

l Grand Lodge of Michigan Constitutions and By-Laws Article XXXI, 4-
215
31 Sec. 2

li http://www.msana.com/focusarchives/focusapr01.asp

lii http://recognitioncommission.org/2004/06/10/the-standards-ofrecognition/

liii http://www.freewebs.com/stelmo70a/aboutus.htm

liv Pike, A., 1871, Morals and Dogma, pg. 5, para. 1 and 2

lv http://www.chandlerlodge227.org/library/Cabletow.pdf

lvi
http://www.wcl760.com/docs/library/Baltimore%20Convention.pdf

lvii Belton, J. 2011, The English Masonic Union of 1813: A Tale of Antient
and Moderns, Arima Publishing

lviii http://www.freemasonry-freemasonry.com/arnaldoGeng.html

lix
http://www.themasonictrowel.com/Articles/History/other_files/ope
rative_freemasonry.htm

lx
http://easternillinoisfreemasonry.blogspot.com/2009/03/clandestinelodge-
beware.html

lxi http://www.nytimes.com/2009/07/03/us/03masons.html?_r=0

lxii
http://www.facebook.com/photo.php?fbid=187939354690868&seta.14
3150659169738.33013.14274495243642&type=1&theater

lxiii
http://www.figstreet.com/guesthouse/simpleweddingceremony.html
#Simple

lxiv Compact between the Most Worshipful Grand Lodge of Texas and
the Most Worshipful Prince Hall Grand Lodge
of Texas and Jurisdiction, F. & A.M., signed April 23, 2007 Donny W.
Broughton and Wilbert M. Curtis, Grand
Masters of both Grand Lodges, respectively.

lxv
http://www.stanford.edu/dept/english/courses/sites/lunsford/page
s/defs.htm

lxvi Micciche, L. 2004, Making a Case for Rhetorical Grammar, National
Council of Teachers of English,
https://www.csun.edu/~bashforth/305_PDF/305_PDF_Grammar/M
akingACaseForRhetoricalGrammar_Micciche.pdf

lxvii Grant, E. 1974, A Source Book in Medieval Science, The Latin
Encyclopedists, Harvard University Press